52 Strategies for

LIFE

LOVE &

WORK

Transforming Your Life One Week at a Time

Anne Grady

Graphic Design by Brenda Hawkes

Edited by Phyllis Jask

Author photos by Netanya Bomani

Printed in the United States of America

ISBN-13: 978-1497593619

ISBN-10: 1497593611

Evan

For showing me the true meaning of unconditional love and teaching me more than I ever thought possible.

Rylee

For your incredible kindness, patience, sense of humor, and love.

Jay

For being my superhero, now and always.

Praise for *52 Strategies for Life, Love & Work*

"By sharing her personal story with humor and sincerity, Anne Grady speaks from the heart about how she used these 52 strategies to make incremental changes in her own life. She provides practical tools to help us make changes that stick."

—*Michelle Smith, Area Director of Human Resources, Omni Hotels*

"Anne Grady is funny, honest, articulate, and inspiring. Her no-nonsense approach increases teamwork, productivity, motivation and smiles."

—*Jenny Magic, Principal/VP of Content Strategy, SiteGoals LLC*

"Spot-on tips which can be used now. Invaluable!"

—*Greg Darthoit, Senior Manager, Dell*

"Anne Grady will take you on a journey that explores the wonders of human nature, unconditional love, and extraordinary self-awareness. Bravo Anne Grady! I am a fan for life."

—*Anne Bruce, Bestselling McGraw-Hill author of more than 20 books, including* Discover True North, Be Your Own Mentor, How to Motivate Every Employee, *and* Speak for a Living

"Her entertaining and candid approach to motivation and goal setting left me feeling inspired to tackle professional and personal challenges with a new mindset."

—*Robbi Craig, Health and Human Services Commission*

"Anne Grady has the exceptional ability to inspire, educate, and entertain…often in a single sentence!"

—*Rose Batson, President, Women's Chamber of Commerce of Texas*

Contents

PART THREE: WORK

Prologue

Evan lunged toward me with scissors and yelled, "I'm going to kill you!"

He was sweating, his blue eyes were filled with rage, and his teeth were clenched. He tried to stab me, but I was able to wrestle the scissors from his grasp. His strength was incredible as the adrenaline surged through his body. As I held him back, he scratched me across the throat and down my arms. He was spitting, biting, and grasping for anything he could reach. We were both out of breath, and I felt like I was trying to contain a wild animal. As small drops of blood began to fall from my neck, I began to sob. I didn't cry because I was being attacked. I cried because the attacker was my three-year-old son.

I held him tightly, both for my safety and his own. He cried, yelled, screamed, spit, kicked, bit, twisted, contorted, and struggled for more than 30 minutes. Then suddenly his small body, that was minutes ago unmanageably strong, sunk and became limp. With a sadness that is unimaginable, he said, "Mommy, uppy. Please pick me up."

What had just happened? How had we gone from giggling and playing to a situation right out of a horror movie? Unfortunately, this was not an isolated incident. This was the kind of meltdown we experienced all too often. Something had to change. I just didn't know where to begin.

Acknowledgments

I am grateful for the most amazing support system. Without these people, I would be lost.

To my friends, thank you for believing in me. I am so fortunate to you have you in my life, and I love you.

To Michael, Tracie, and the rest of Evan's support team, thank you for your relentless patience, support, and love. You have given us the faith to stay strong.

To Jan, Phyllis, Brenda, Susan, and Anne, thank you for making this book a reality.

To my mom, you are my hero and my friend. Your unconditional love, strength, and selflessness are beyond amazing. Thank you for believing in me and for being here every step of the way. I love you with all of my heart.

To my husband Jay, there are no words to express how much I admire you, respect you, and love you. Thank you for being my cheerleader, for believing in our family, and for your incredible strength and support. I'm looking forward to the next four decades. I love you.

To my daughter Rylee, I am so grateful you are in my life. Thank you for your courage, your patience, and for loving us, even if we are a little crazy.

To my love bug Evan, I am incredibly blessed to be your mom, and I am so proud of the person you have become. I love you up to God and back.

Finally, to all of the families who are affected by mental illness—you are not alone.

About the Author

Anne Grady is living proof that making tough changes can have monumental results. As a nationally recognized speaker, author, and consultant, Anne candidly shares her own journey and the lessons she's learned to help organizations, and the people in them, achieve lasting results.

As Founder and President of Acclivity Performance and the Anne Grady Group, Anne works with a diverse array of companies, not-for-profits, government agencies, and individuals, and uses her unparalleled ability to help her audiences implement solutions for the real issues they face every day. Anne helps guide organizations toward changes that build teamwork, increase productivity, and reduce stress. Anne incorporates the very mantras she champions professionally into her personal life to work through the challenges she faces each day as mom of two, one with special needs. With her signature style of wit and candor, Anne helps people transform the way they approach life, love, and work.

Anne holds a master's degree in Organizational Communication. She lives in Round Rock, Texas, with her husband, two children, and their "therapy" dogs Bernie and Charlie.

For details on how to bring the strategies in this book into your organization, or to learn about the other organizational development solutions available, contact Anne at (512) 821-1111 or email her at anne@annegradygroup.com. You can also visit her online at www.annegradygroup.com for information, scheduling press interviews, availability, and fees.

Keep in touch by sharing your success stories with Anne!

 www.annegradygroup.com/facebook

 www.annegradygroup.com/linkedin

 www.annegradygroup.com/youtube

 www.annegradygroup.com/blog

 @annegradygroup

Introduction

We all play multiple roles—mother, father, sister, child, student, employee, whatever. We live. We love. We work. Hopefully in most of our experiences we feel happy, grateful, and content. But at some point along the way, there are bound to be circumstances that we'd just rather not be in: financial challenge, heartache, illness, a horrible boss, or any other situation that forces us to tap into resources we probably didn't even know we had. True, some of us have bigger challenges than others at different times in our lives, but everyone experiences turmoil and tumult. For me, having a son with severe mental illness forced me to dig into the depths of my soul to find the strength to persevere. Don't get me wrong, I've had my share of "Why me?" or "This just isn't fair" moments. Many have told me that God would not give me more than I can handle. I can tell you right now, God has way too much confidence in me. But having Evan in my life is the driving force behind my own personal trek toward transformation. I quickly learned that if I do what I've always done, I'll get what I've always gotten. And what I was getting wasn't working.

I've written this collection of 52 strategies to help you transform your communication, productivity, attitude, and overall results, just like I did. Why 52 strategies? Because the changes we make need to be subtle if they are going to be sustainable. Ever tried to lose weight only to gain it back? How many New Year's resolutions have you made that petered out by February? Change challenges our comfortable habits, and it only happens one of three ways: rarely, slowly, or never. If you break these 52 strategies down into more manageable weekly chunks, you can succeed at making the changes you want in your life, one week at a time. After each strategy, I will list things that you can do—*immediately*—that will inspire you take action.

I've broken the 52 strategies into three sections that can apply to the different parts of your life: life, love, work. That's not to say that strategies in one part of the book can't be used in another part of your life—they can and should! You play many roles throughout any given day. It's impossible to leave work at home or home at work. You blend areas of your life into each other, and that's the way it should be. Your personal relationships will absolutely affect your relationships at work, just as your professional relationships will affect your relationships at home.

Part One: Life focuses on your personal growth and development. Most of our thoughts and behaviors come from how we see ourselves, which affects how we perceive the world.

Part Two: Love provides strategies for all of your relationships. Whether they are personal or professional relationships, they all involve your heart as well as your mind.

Part Three: Work identifies ways that you can work smarter, not harder, to improve productivity, define your priorities, and chart the course for your life.

You'll find a combination of tactical, hands-on strategies blended with insight and inspiration within these pages. Each chapter has a Slight Edge Strategy section that suggests ways to adopt these changes in your own life. Work on one strategy each week. I'll share how I used these strategies I learned from textbooks to become fundamental building blocks of my life.

Trust me, my life isn't always daisies, butterflies, and rainbows. After experiencing the trauma of Evan's daily, multiple meltdowns, I knew

I wouldn't be able to continue in crisis mode. Something had to change. So I carefully examined all the things I was teaching about how to make one's life work and applied them to my own life. Any of it that couldn't help me through my circumstances was thrown into the discard pile, and everything that did help became a life raft. It's really easy to tout a philosophy like "Be Proactive, Not Reactive" when it's just a matter of finishing a project on time or dealing with a cranky coworker. But when you're really struggling—when someone you love is sick or you're in chronic pain, or when addiction, unemployment, divorce, or death of a loved one seems to take over your life—internalizing a simple philosophy can keep you from falling to pieces. And it can keep you calm and happy, moving forward in the midst of the storm you're in.

You don't have to be going through crisis or face similar challenges to the next guy reading this book. You do have to be willing to look in the mirror and examine what you are currently doing that is working and not working in your life. And you have to be willing to try new tools for what may be old—even comfortably familiar—problems and habits.

■ ■ ■

I also wrote this book to bring mental illness out of the shadows. I feel so strongly about this that I'm donating a portion of my book proceeds to National Alliance on Mental Illness (NAMI). Mental illness affects one in four adults and one in 10 children in the United States,[1] yet in any given year, only 20 percent of children with mental illness are identified and receive treatment.

When a child shoots up a school, we are shocked and wonder how this could possibly happen. As long as attitudes and stigmas toward

---

[1]National Alliance on Mental Illness, www.nami.org.

mental health treatment remain, and treatment stays expensive and difficult to find, the tragic stories will continue to be told.

Today, Evan is 11 years old. I love him more than I thought I could ever love someone, but his illness has wreaked havoc on our family. In November 2010, my husband Jay—Evan's stepfather—and I checked him into the pediatric psych unit at Children's Medical Center in Dallas for two months. Hospitalizing Evan was the most difficult decision we had ever made, but also the best one. Evan, by that point, had been diagnosed with bipolar disorder, oppositional defiant disorder, frontal lobe deficits, ADHD, cerebral dysrhythmia, and sensory integration problems. His treatment team was phenomenal, and Jay and I learned new ways to handle his aggression and new approaches to manage his behavior. When we returned home from the hospital, I had a new understanding about how using the 52 strategies I had been teaching had kept me somewhat sane over the years.

I make no secret that I still struggle daily. I still get horrible phone calls from Evan's school, and we still manage extreme behaviors on an hourly and daily basis. The doctors have told us one of three things will happen: he will get better, he will get worse, or he will stay the same. All have the same odds. Having a child with mental illness is the hardest, scariest, most taxing, and most humbling experience of my life.

I have found that these 52 strategies bring order, peace, and happiness to my work life, my home life, my love life, and everything in between. And I am passionate about providing tools and resources to help other people do the same. Using these strategies has been my life line. They have changed my life, my work, and the way I love, and I am confident they can do the same for you.

Part One:

STRATEGY 1:
Succeed with Slight Edge Changes

We've all done it. We wake up one morning and announce that, starting now, we're going to get organized, lose weight, increase our savings, de-clutter our desk. We make an honest attempt to completely transform our lives. A few days later, we're back on the sofa in front of the TV, next to a pile of unfolded laundry, eating a cheeseburger, finishing out the day with a pint of Ben & Jerry's.

The truth is it's easy to make a big change initially, only to find ourselves right back where we started. That's because behavior change happens in one of three ways: rarely, slowly, or never. Successful change requires small shifts over a long time.

Most of us have more than enough on our plates without making huge changes that require additional thought, preparation, and time, and may throw our life's rhythm into chaos. I know in our house, just getting Evan ready for school is arduous and difficult. I must say, "No, stop it…Please don't…That's not acceptable…We don't do that…That's not allowed…That hurts the dog…Don't say that…Get that out of your mouth…No, you can't pee on the cat…" 200 times before we even reach 7:00 am.

By the time the kids are at school, it's time to Tweet, Like, comment to my Facebook friends that their babies are adorable, have a meeting (or four), speak at a conference, write a blog post, walk the dog, pick up the dry cleaning, do the grocery shopping, cook dinner, clean the kitchen, make lunches for tomorrow, put the kids to bed, and on and on, and somehow still have the libido to keep my marriage sizzling. Then it's time to wake up in just a few hours to do it all again.

Slight Edge Equals Taking Baby Steps

I couldn't imagine making some of the changes I wanted to make and still being able to keep up with it all. Then I discovered the beauty of the Slight Edge.[2] Slight Edge means incremental changes over time. It means we don't take some drastic action that will use up all our time and resources; we just take baby steps toward our goal. For instance:

- Increase productivity by 30 minutes a day and we've added 23 days a year.

- Alter the thermostat by two degrees and we save 5 percent on our energy bill.

- Cut out one soda a day for a year and we'll lose 10 pounds.

I was ecstatic when I learned the concept of Slight Edge because that's something *I could do*! I could succeed at that. Even better, the pay-off for a slight push rather than a life revolution is much bigger than it looks from the starting gate. In a horse or car race, the difference between first place and second place can be milliseconds; hence the term "won by a nose." But the difference in payout is huge! That's true of Slight Edge. It's not the big things we do one time that make the difference. It is the little changes we make, consistently over a long time, that bring the biggest payoff.

Recently I read an article in the *Philadelphia Daily News*[3] about a New Jersey woman who lost 75 pounds over three years. She ate normal food, although she did trade candy bars for protein bars and nixed her two-soda-a-day habit. She didn't join a gym or have anything sewn up or sucked out. She just bought a pedometer for $10 at Walmart. Peggy Bradford had heard that if you want to lose weight, you need to take 10,000 steps a day. So she started between 6,000 and 10,000 and has built up to about 30,000 steps a day. She jogs in place while she does paperwork, dishes, irons, and when she watches TV.

---

[2] Jeff Olson, *The Slight Edge: Turning Simple Disciplines into Massive Success* (Lake Dallas, TX: Success Books, 2005).

[3] Jenice Armstrong, "Peggy Bradford of Sewell, N.J., loses 75 pounds," *Philadelphia Daily News*, December 31, 2012, available at www.philly.com/philly/columnists/jenice_armstrong/20121231_Jenice_Armstrong_Peggy_Bradford_of_Sewell_N_J_loses_75_pounds.html.

She's lost the weight. She's kept it off. And she's made this exercise a part of how she lives every day. She built gradual and subtle change into her life.

She didn't do those things all at once and neither can we. Even if we were perched on a mountaintop with nothing to do but create change within ourselves, we couldn't do it because what needs to change is the way we operate in the busy, demanding, ever-changing reality of our lives. Taking one strategy at a time, working on it for a while, and applying it to every situation that fits will eventually create for us a new way of functioning.

What is one thing you've wanted to accomplish but have been putting off, or one behavior or habit you've wanted to change? It doesn't even have to be a big thing. If you want to get healthier, it could be taking 2,000 steps a day. If you want to save money, go without one thing you would have otherwise purchased that day. ***Keep it simple!*** Trying to accomplish everything at once is overwhelming and unrealistic. Too much change too fast equals no change at all.

What one thing do you want to work on this week? Is it something at work or at home, or could it be something you do that's strictly for you?

SLIGHT EDGE STRATEGY

- **Identify a change:** Identify one change you'd like to make in your life. Think about how you can apply a Slight Edge Strategy—a small change—that will incrementally add up to a big difference. For example, I did this with swimming. I used to hate exercise. Swimming was the only exercise I could stand, but I didn't have access to a pool. When we moved into our new house, the neighborhood pool was literally right down the street. I started swimming three or four times a week. I started with five laps, then six, then 10; now I'm up to 30. I have lost 25 pounds, and I look and feel better than I have since college.

- **Track your progress:** How are you going to keep track of your success? Will you track your progress on an app? Keep a written diary?

- **Create a visual reminder:** What steps will you keep in place to track your progress and success? (I once heard of a woman who, during a drastic weight loss effort, kept a stick of butter in the freezer to visualize every quarter pound she lost.)

STRATEGY 2: Stop Reacting

If all you have is a hammer, everything looks like a nail.

—Abraham Maslow

All our lives we've been building neurological highways, paths that are so deep, smooth, and well-worn, that certain thoughts travel from point A to point B faster than lightning. These are our reactions. We might have been born with some of them. Others we were taught. They are our unprocessed responses to fear, stress, threat, anxiety, failure, and even affection.

It's kind of like a game of pool. Hit one ball, and it affects all of the others. The ball doesn't know where it's going; it's simply following the rules of physics. We have our own internal rules for how to respond to things, and unless we stop to really think about it, we are probably no smarter about how we're handling it than that pool ball.

We spend an inordinate amount of time reacting. Think about it: I bet that in the last 24 hours you can think of at least one or two situations, conversations, or issues that have caused you to react in a way that wasn't as productive as you would have liked. It could have been as simple as rolling your eyes and sighing when you saw that certain number on your caller ID. Unfortunately, it's a self-perpetuating cycle. Reaction begets reaction and like that pool ball, we may end up bonking into all kinds of obstacles before we ever reach a solution.

Reaction in Action

For me, the reaction ditch I fell into every time was reacting to Evan's outbursts. Here's my child, my beautiful boy whom I love, who suddenly can become this aggressive, abusive kid who hates me. He calls me horrible names. Threatens to kill me. Tells me he wishes I were dead. This tore my heart out every time. When he would lunge at me and attack me, I would burst into tears.

Who wouldn't? It would freak me out if a stranger on the street did that. Here is someone who has complete access to my heart, whom I fed, dressed, bathed, snuggled, and nursed back to health when he was sick. How could he treat me like this?

Every time, my internal reaction was betrayal and heartbreak. Never once did it improve the situation.

Finally, when Evan was admitted to the hospital, I accepted that these rages weren't about me. They were about his illness. My reaction might have made a difference if Evan were a normal kid just expressing one of those experimental "I hate yous." But that wasn't the case. I needed to stop reacting and come up with a strategy for handling the rages.

We began to help Evan identify coping strategies. Things like squeezing silly putty, taking deep breaths, or counting to 100. While those things didn't work every time, they certainly helped us make progress. It was a strategy. Strategy is the alternative to reaction.

Think about this: a situation arises, and instead of yelling, quitting, blaming, or justifying, just stop to think:

- **What just happened?**

- **Why did it happen?**

- **What can I do about it that will positively affect the outcome of this situation?**

- **How can I respond effectively when situations like this arise in the future?**

A reaction is our unconscious, habitual approach, but a strategy is a consciously chosen approach that fits the situation, individual, or personal history. A strategy is deliberate, and so are the results.

Learning to think proactively and strategically about our lives is a lot of work. It's changing an ingrained way of living and a bunch of old habits. While developing a more strategic approach to life requires more effort on the front end, it is invaluable to our long game. If it were easy, everyone would have various tools to use to communicate flawlessly, manage their time easily, and exist in a perpetual state of happiness. Lord knows that's simply not the case.

Developing the strategy is the easy part. Implementing it is the tricky part. There's a huge difference between knowing something and actually doing it. If we've got a set of good strategies and we live by them, we can change our lives.

Everything's not a nail. Some things require more than just a hammer. It's about acquiring—and using—the right tools in our tool box.

SLIGHT EDGE STRATEGY

- **Stop reacting:** Where have you been reacting in a negative way in your personal or professional life? Could it be something your manager says or does that triggers a negative response? Maybe it's something at home that your partner does that just ticks you off? Ask yourself what you can do about it that will positively affect the outcome.

- **Identify a strategy:** Identify one coping strategy that can minimize your reaction. Count to 10? Ask yourself questions before you speak? Take a time-out before responding to a situation?

- **Practice makes perfect:** It might take some trial and error, but you can find strategies that will work.

STRATEGY 3: Realize Your Courage

Whether we're defending a conviction, confronting a coworker or neighbor about difficult behavior, coping with a challenging situation, or simply hanging on when it would be easier to let go, courage comes in all shapes and sizes.

Is there something you've wanted to try, but fear stopped you? Is there an uncomfortable conversation you're avoiding? Is there a decision that you need to make but you're anxious about the consequences? If so, I'm here to give you a little nudge and encourage you to be courageous, in whatever way makes the most sense for you.

How much time do we spend being fearful? I'm not talking about monsters-in-the-closet scared, but how much time do we spend being afraid of the unknown? We're worried about what will happen with the financial market, our job, whether our kids will turn out all right, or whether our projects will earn us the respect we seek at work.

So many of us live out fantasies in our heads about good or bad things that *might* happen—most of which never happen. It is said that 95 percent of what we're afraid of never even happens, and the other 5 percent are things we can't control. We spend an inordinate amount of energy focusing on the *what ifs*. Have you ever paid attention to how much time you spend worrying about things that might happen?

There's been a lot of focus in recent years about the emotional and physical health benefits of mindfulness; that is, living very consciously in what's really happening *right now*: Right now, I'm not homeless, I'm

Courage doesn't always roar. Sometimes courage is the quiet voice at the end of the day saying, "I will try again tomorrow."—*Mary Anne Radmacher*

living in a nice home. Right now, my kids are safe. Right now, I'm healthy and capable. If I need to take action I can, but just being afraid about it isn't actually doing anything except making me miserable. In fact, a tenet of many religions is the idea that we create much of our own misery in our thoughts.

Courage isn't the absence of fear. We all feel fear. Courage is finding ways to deal with that fear productively. There's often the most amazing rush of joy and energy when we face something we're afraid of. That's why so many people are drawn to extreme sports or taking risks. They feel the fear, just like everybody else. But they've learned that facing it and doing what they set out to do gives them an unbelievable sense of accomplishment. And that's worth the moments of fear beforehand.

When fighting fear, keep these things in mind:

1. **Everyone is feeling the same way:** Have you ever been to a party or networking event where you didn't know very many people? Chances are that you felt anxious, nervous, and hesitant to join conversations. Well, you are certainly not alone. A lot of people dread networking events (me included). How did you meet all of the people you now consider friends? You were introduced, probably felt a bit awkward at first, but did it anyway.

2. **A little fear is a good thing:** I often get asked how I can get up in front of thousands of people and speak without being nervous. My comment is always, "What makes you think I'm not nervous?" Of course I'm nervous. Anyone would be nervous. The trick isn't getting rid of the nerves, it's channeling the energy in the right direction. We all need a little adrenaline boost every now and then.

3. **Look for the right things:** We usually find what we're looking for. If we're looking for all the reasons things will be awful, we are going to find them. Instead, look for the positive. I had to chuckle at a recent conference where I was speaking about the power of attitude. A woman approached me afterward and said, "I'm an eternal optimist, but nothing good ever comes of it!"

4. **If you're not uncomfortable, you're not getting better:** You are all here to grow, learn, and continuously improve. If you're always in your comfort zone, you never push yourself to get better. If you always know all the answers and always feel comfortable, chances are, you are missing opportunities to take yourself to the next level.

5. **Don't borrow from tomorrow:** My mom says this to me every time I start to catastrophize about Evan and what our future will look like; this is one I've had to work very hard at. Spend your time, effort, and energy on things you can control today. Worrying about tomorrow won't change what *might* happen.

SLIGHT EDGE STRATEGY

- **Stop inventing catastrophe:** Pay attention to how much time you spend cooking up scary scenarios in your brain. When you notice it happening, focus on what's really going on in the moment. Chances are it's not anywhere near as bad as what you have created in your mind.

- **Embrace the scary moment:** This is an opportunity to grow as a person and experience a little jolt of triumph when you've overcome your fear. What is your plan to embrace it?

- **Identify what's been holding you back:** Identify one fear that has been preventing you from accomplishing what you want. Can you pinpoint what triggers it? How can you overcome this fear?

- **Don't borrow from tomorrow:** Don't waste your energy on things that you can't control. Worrying about what might happen tomorrow won't do you any good today.

STRATEGY 4: Readjust Your Attitude

I t was late February and miserably cold and rainy. I had been having a horrible time with Evan. He was in preschool, and he was getting extremely aggressive with the teachers and other kids. Up until then he had reserved most of his aggression for me. I was a divorced single mom at the time, trying to manage a full-time consulting practice, and I was exhausted.

So the fact that I'd just arrived to give a 90-minute keynote presentation about the power of attitude and positive thinking struck me as particularly ironic. This was clear evidence to me that God has a twisted sense of humor.

I gathered my thoughts, went in, and talked for an hour and a half about the power of attitude and positivity. Then I got back in my car and sobbed.

Now, I'm a big supporter of a good cry now and then. But this wasn't that. This was defeat. I didn't understand at the time what I was up against with Evan. I hadn't come to terms with the fact that his illness was real. This was my life now. No amount of crying, complaining, or self-pity would change that. I could talk a good game about positive attitude, but as long as my circumstances were this hard, I didn't think anybody had a right to ask me to have one myself.

The truth is, I had all the skills to change my attitude. I knew what I should do. I just wasn't able, or more importantly *willing*, to do it.

The Improvement Trifecta

I see this all the time in organizations for which I consult, speak, and train. They spend countless dollars on training and development to "fix" deficient skills like customer service, conflict management, productivity, leadership, and communication.

Although training is essential for transferring skills and knowledge, it often falls short of inspiring people to actually use the skills they've learned. For a person, a marriage, a parent, a manager, a customer service representative, or anyone else to actually improve, we must have a combination of three things:

1. **Skill:** The "How"

2. **Activity:** The "What"

3. **Attitude:** The "Why" and the "Want to"

We might know how to communicate well with our boss or spouse, and we might even do it consistently. But when we're tired, fed up, and frustrated, and our boss or spouse says something that makes us want to replay a scene from a slasher film, no amount of skill is going to help us.

Attitude Defined

Now take that fed-up mood and stretch it over a long time. That's an attitude. When it comes to attitudes, we usually hear someone has a good one, a bad one, or they just plain have one. An attitude is nothing more than a habit of thought. It is a habitual way of thinking about something.

It doesn't matter if someone is capable of great customer service if he thinks his company doesn't treat him well and he's resentful all day at work. It doesn't matter if someone knows how to manage people if she's mad she didn't get to choose her team and wants to demonstrate to her bosses that this team is no good.

And it wouldn't have made much difference for me to know the strategies I needed with Evan as long as I was feeling sorry for myself that I had to use these strategies in the first place.

Once we've got a bad attitude, we see everything through crap-colored glasses.

It finally hit me that my situation wasn't going to change on its own. Whatever it was that was going on with Evan, it wasn't going away. Being mad or sad or resentful wasn't changing it. The only change I could affect, the only control I did have, was the way I reacted and responded.

I could learn strategies that would mitigate the problem. I could use them consistently. And I could decide to wake up every morning glad to be alive and feel grateful that I had the means and ability to be able to do something to help my kiddo cope with the storm he was living in every day.

And doing that changed my life. I had no idea what weight I had added to the already heavy load I carried just by throwing a big ol' resentful attitude on top of it.

Attitude really is everything. And no one has control of yours but you.

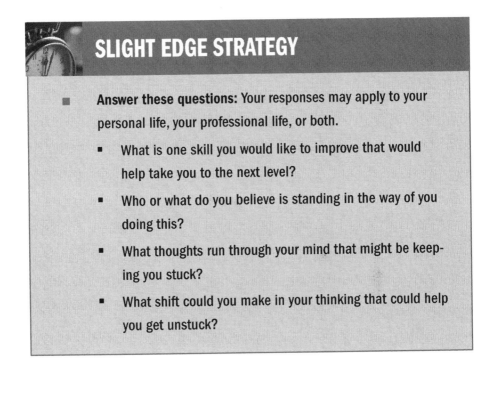

SLIGHT EDGE STRATEGY

- **Answer these questions:** Your responses may apply to your personal life, your professional life, or both.

  - What is one skill you would like to improve that would help take you to the next level?

  - Who or what do you believe is standing in the way of you doing this?

  - What thoughts run through your mind that might be keeping you stuck?

  - What shift could you make in your thinking that could help you get unstuck?

STRATEGY 5: Get Unstuck

Brushing our teeth. Smoking. Exercise. Stress. Bathing. Emotional eating. Gratitude. Negativity.

What do all of these things have in common? Good or bad, they are all habits. In fact, a huge chunk of how we live is dictated by habit. More than 45 percent of our responses, thoughts, and actions are so habituated, they don't require conscious thought.[4]

Trying to change one of these habits seems like it should be easy: Just stop. Or start. But it isn't easy…it's hard. Why? Because most of us don't realize that the battle for changing habits isn't in our doing, it's in our thinking. Habits come from ways of thinking—conditioning—that cause us to behave the way we do or hold the attitudes we have. We often talk about attitude, but what we really mean is the habitual way that we think about things.

Our brains are fascinating. Different parts process different things. For example, the basal ganglia are associated with processes like movement, learning, and habits; similarly, the cerebellum plays a role in cognitive functions like emotions and processing memories. It's easy for the brain to use these areas; they don't require much effort. Problem solving, critical thinking, and more difficult tasks take place in the pre-frontal cortex, and our brains have to work much harder in these areas. Our brains will take any repeated behavior and turn it into a habit. Fortunately, we have some control over the ability to re-train our brains: it's called self-directed neuroplasticity.

We are conditioned from birth by parents, teachers, friends, relatives, and anyone we spend a considerable amount of time around. Most powerfully, we condition ourselves. By consistently thinking about

---

[4]Charles Duhigg, *The Power of Habit: Why We Do What We Do in Life and Business* (New York: Random House, 2012).

circumstances, people, and situations in a particular way, we reinforce our own attitudes and conditioning.

The way we think dictates the way we act and behave, the way we act and behave determines our results, and our results determine our level of success.

Let's take a fairly generic example: dieting. We've all probably tried the following: drinking more water, exercising, eating healthier foods, decreasing sugar and carbs, etc. These are all good things to do to promote weight loss. If, while we are doing these things, we're telling ourselves that we're starving, that we're suffering, that we're eating food only fit for a rabbit and torturing our poor bodies into submission, we are very likely to fail.

We're creating a situation where our own thoughts are adding a huge burden to the task we're trying to accomplish: *This is exhausting... I hate that food...that exercise is awkward...I should take a day off because this might not be healthy...So-and-So never exercises and she's fine...* It would be like performing a task at work with our boss yelling at us the whole time.

That's why nutritionists agree that diets don't work. We have to change our lifestyles and eating habits.

Our thoughts travel down neural pathways. And our habitual thoughts have traveled down the same paths so long and so often it's like wagon wheel ruts on the Oregon Trail. So it can be really difficult to create new neural pathways around the same ideas—like exercise is fun and rewarding instead of boring and time consuming. We literally have to force ourselves to think differently about something over and over and over again. And because it's hard work, it's best if we can only limit it to one skill at a time. Imagine trying to learn how to do a new job while being a new parent and working on an MBA—that's just too much for any one person to handle.

So when we learn new ways to handle stress, manage projects, or manage conflict, we have to focus hard and practice those skills over and over in order to build new neural pathways for our thoughts to travel down. This is self-directed neuroplasticity. It takes a lot of mental energy. It's also where the magic happens. To help you get started getting unstuck:

1. **Define success and write it down:** How will you know the changes you have made have been successful? Where do you want to end up? Be specific about this. The more clearly you can define success, the better chance you have of accomplishing it. Now, write it down. Regardless of how clearly you think, writing your thoughts down helps you crystallize them. Make a very vivid picture or story about what the new results will look like. This is a powerful exercise and can determine the success of your outcome. You can even do this in the form of a dream board (see Strategy 7 for more on creating your own dream board).

2. **Work backward:** Whatever result you are currently getting is stemming from your actions and behaviors. Spend some time paying attention to the thoughts that occur when those behaviors arise. Make note of them, especially the ones that pop up time and again.

3. **Create a replacement thought:** Most people try to go from a negative to a positive thought, but for most of us that's too much of a stretch. Try going from a negative thought to a neutral thought. Dr. David Burns does a great job of explaining this in his book *Feeling Good*.[5] For example, when I find myself thinking "Why me? Why do I have to deal with this situation?" I use the replacement thought: "It is what it is." I have this saying displayed everywhere so I'm constantly reminded of it.

4. **Make visual reminders:** Visual reminders are extremely helpful. In my car, I have a rabbit's foot that I've had since I was a little girl to remind me I'm lucky. In my office, I have a little Buddha on my desk to remind myself to feel peace. And on my refrigerator, I have fortune cookie papers that have a meaningful message. If you've already created one, look to your dream board. See where it is you want to be or who it is you want to become.

---

[5]David D. Burns, *Feeling Good: The New Mood Therapy*, rev. ed. (New York: Harper Collins. 1999).

5.   **Talk to yourself rather than listen to yourself:** Most of us have those little annoying, self-defeating messages swirling around our heads. Rather than listening to them, replace them with deliberate messages that are positive and reaffirming.

Let's apply a real example. Most of us struggle to meet all of our deadlines and check off everything on our to-do lists. What behaviors are contributing to the problem? Is it procrastination? Poor organization? Lack of clearly defined goals or expectations? Where do those behaviors come from? They may come from thinking, "I can't get this all done!" or "I'm so overwhelmed!" or maybe even, "Why am I working harder than everyone else?" Now it's time for replacement statements like, "I plan and prioritize my day and do one thing at a time." or "All I can do is all I can do." or "I clarify expectations from my boss to make sure I'm focused on high priority activities and tasks."

Creating new habits is certainly not easy, but the process is pretty straightforward, and it is doable. Getting in a rut is dangerous; after all, a rut is just a grave with no ends. Where do you need to get unstuck?

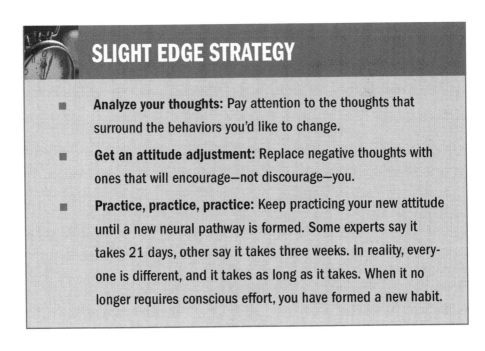

SLIGHT EDGE STRATEGY

■   **Analyze your thoughts:** Pay attention to the thoughts that surround the behaviors you'd like to change.

■   **Get an attitude adjustment:** Replace negative thoughts with ones that will encourage—not discourage—you.

■   **Practice, practice, practice:** Keep practicing your new attitude until a new neural pathway is formed. Some experts say it takes 21 days, other say it takes three weeks. In reality, everyone is different, and it takes as long as it takes. When it no longer requires conscious effort, you have formed a new habit.

STRATEGY 6: Escape Your Comfort Zone

Life begins at the end of your comfort zone.

—Neale Donald Walsch

A few months after our stay at the hospital, Evan continued to do really well. He was getting positive daily reports from school, he was doing great in his social skills classes, and his behavior was more manageable than ever before. His behavior hadn't arrived at this place by magic. After intense therapy, we had gotten really vigilant about staying on top of his behaviors, sticking to our routine, and tracking everything that happened like weather scientists tracking a potential hurricane. Then we got comfortable—too comfortable.

Because things were going well, we got lazy and slid back into the comfort zone, letting behaviors go without addressing them, failing to track our progress, and morphing the schedule. Unfortunately, we were reminded how dangerous that can be. We had to virtually start over, go back to basics, and become once again vigilant about staying more focused, disciplined, and consistent.

We were in the habit of living the way we lived before. Like falling onto the sofa in front of our favorite TV show with a bag of chips, it felt so effortless to fall back into our comfort zone and old habits. We'd spent months reconditioning ourselves around managing Evan's behavior, but it was still amazing how fast we fell into old habits.

Most people don't get stronger, smarter, or happier in their comfort zone; in fact they don't grow at all. A comfort zone sounds like such a pleasant place to be, but people who are in them all the time are generally stuck. And getting stuck there occurs so gradually, sometimes it's hard to realize it's even happening.

It's all too easy to get complacent at work, with our kids, in our relationships, and even with ourselves. It's hard to remember and even harder to practice, but the great things in life typically happen because we stretch out of our comfort zone.

We've talked about the challenge of changing our thoughts. Although that's the most important piece of the puzzle, we have to actually change our behaviors as well. Getting what we want requires effort. It requires us to go beyond what's comfortable and forces us to work for it.

Are there areas of your life where you have gotten complacent or where you could benefit by getting out of your comfort zone? Are there habits that are keeping you stuck? The interesting thing about habits is that you can't get rid of one without taking on a different one to replace it. Until a new thought or behavior becomes so ingrained and habitual that we do it without even thinking about it, we stay stuck in our old patterns.

The poem on the following page by an anonymous author captures it perfectly.

It's hard to remember and even harder to practice, but the great things in life typically happen because we stretch out of our comfort zone.

I am your constant companion.

I am your greatest helper or heaviest burden.

I will push you onward or drag you down to failure.

I am completely at your command.

Half of the things you do you might as well turn over to me and I will do them—quickly and correctly.

I am easily managed—you must be firm with me.

Show me exactly how you want something done and after a few lessons, I will do it automatically.

I am the servant of great people,

and alas, of all failures as well.

Those who are great, I have made great.

Those who are failures, I have made failures.

I am not a machine though.

I work with the precision of a machine plus the intelligence of a person.

You may run me for profit or run me for ruin— it makes no difference to me.

Take me, train me, be firm with me, and

I will place the world at your feet.

Be easy with me and I will destroy you.

Who am I?

I am Habit.

However comfortable a habit may be, if it's a negative habit, it usually causes us some pain. It's much easier to stay comfortable with old problems than be uncomfortable with new solutions. The pain has to be uncomfortable enough to inspire us to take action. And sometimes because the behavior and the pain are habitual and therefore feel "normal," it may take time to identify them.

Frequently, it's easiest to spot those pain points in the moment we experience them: In the moment someone else speaks an idea we had in a meeting because we're not accustomed to speaking up; in the moment we realize we can't pay a bill because we didn't budget; in the moment we realize we didn't spend quality time with our kids...again. Instead of avoiding the pain of those moments, let them instruct us:

- How did I act or behave that could have caused or contributed to this result?

- How is this pain connected to my comfort zone?

- What habitual thoughts contributed to that behavior?

- What thoughts can I cultivate to support a new behavior?

- How can I act on that new behavior?

SLIGHT EDGE STRATEGY

- **Take a risk:** This week, stop embracing your comfort zone and get comfortable being uncomfortable. Getting what you want requires effort on your part.

- **Let pain points inspire you to action:** Pay attention to your pain points at the moment they happen. Let them instruct you on how to act or think.

- **Keep realistic expectations:** Remember Slight Edge. Make your changes gradually.

STRATEGY 7: Define Success

If you don't know where you're headed, any road will get you there. —*Lewis Carroll*

We arrived at the hospital in Dallas for Evan's treatment in shock, scared, and extremely uncertain of what the future would hold for us. Was this going to be our new normal? Were we going to have to find a place for Evan to live to keep him and everyone around him safe? We didn't even know what to hope for in terms of an outcome. What would success look like?

Later, one of Evan's therapists asked me how I would define success. I knew, because it was what I wished for every day: We wouldn't have daily physical attacks. I would be able to take Evan out in public. We would feel safe in our own home. The therapist told me to go home, go through magazines, and cut out pictures to make a collage that reminded me of this—my dream board. I thought she was crazy.

It turns out that we're all a little crazy. And it wasn't a crazy idea at all. Simply going through the exercise made me clarify what we were trying to accomplish. And having a clear picture of our ideal future gave me inspiration to keep going when things got difficult. I made a dream board, and I love it. It reminds me that where I am today isn't where I have to stay.

Usually, we have some idea where we're headed. We're going to the store to buy this week's groceries. We're going to the office to pitch that new campaign. But when it comes to looking at where we're headed in the long-term, sometimes we're afraid or tell ourselves we are too busy to even stop to think about that. The question "What do I want my life to look like?" is enormous and scary. But let's face it, we're choosing our direction every day, every hour. It's just that frequently, we don't have an ultimate destination in mind.

Have you ever looked in the mirror and wondered where the last 10 years have gone? If you're anything like me, most parts are hanging about an inch lower than they used to, and there are dimples and wrinkles where there should never, ever be dimples and wrinkles.

Most of us go about our lives caught up in day-to-day activity and without knowing it, years go by and we are no closer to accomplishing our goals. Or worse yet, we haven't taken time to set goals at all. All too often, we land somewhere, draw a bull's eye around ourselves, and declare it a victory rather than deliberately taking time to identify where we want to end up and creating a clear path to get there.

That's why I love my dream board. If I start to drift, it brings me back. *That's* what I'm working for. That's what this day is about.

Make your own dream or vision board. Surf Google Images or go through old magazines, pictures, books, and other things lying around the house, and cut out pictures or sayings that represent what you want your life to look like. For example, if you want to vacation on a relaxing beach, add a picture of blue water and white sand to your board. If you see a picture of the man or woman of your dreams, put that on your board as well (unless you are currently in a relationship, in which case, this may be awkward!). Allow yourself to dream big.

Be forewarned: Oftentimes when you let yourself really dwell on what you want, self-defeating thoughts emerge: *That's not going to happen…You're too (fill in negative adjective) to have that…You shouldn't hope for that, you'll only wind up disappointed…Aim for something smaller, instead.*

An exercise that should be inspiring and fun can wind up depressing and hard. If you prepare yourself, you can head off those thoughts before they squash your resolve. Be ready to meet those self-defeating thoughts by focusing on the moment and on your dreams. Staying in the moment, in what you're trying to accomplish, will help you through the rough patches.

You may ask, why not keep my dream board focused on things I know I can attain? The fact is most of us try to plan our dreams around what we think is possible, not what we really desire to achieve. I don't think the problem for most of us is that we set our goals too high and miss. I think the problem is that we set our goals too low and hit them.

When we set aspiring goals, we often fail to pursue them until we know how we're going to achieve them. Fortunately, that's not the way your brain works. When you decide what you want, your brain automatically works backwards and creates thought patterns and ideas you wouldn't have had otherwise. You begin to make conscious and subconscious decisions that will allow you to work toward your goal.

So when you're making your dream board and planning what you want your life to look like, be bold. Give yourself permission to want what you want without letting your inner critic pare it down to the next rung above where you are today.

SLIGHT EDGE STRATEGY

- **Create a dream board:** Choose images that will help you visualize your goals. Display it somewhere where you will see it often. Think about what success looks like in each of the following areas:
  - Attitude
  - Family
  - Finances
  - Career
  - Education
  - Social life
  - Personal growth

STRATEGY 8: Get Inspired

In life, you need either inspiration or desperation.
—*Anthony Robbins*

In life, in order to make a change, we either need to be inspired or we need to be so desperate to change that we're willing to be uncomfortable in order to get to where we want to go. It's great to change because someone or something comes along to lift our sights and get us moving. All too frequently it's desperation, rather than inspiration, that causes us to tackle a difficult change. And that's all right, too.

Have you heard the joke about how many psychiatrists it takes to screw in a light bulb? One, but the light bulb has to really *want* to change.

Then there's the parable about Earl and Bubba, two old hillbillies sitting on the porch in their rocking chairs reminiscing about the good ol' days. In between them sits a big, old hound dog. Every so often, the hound dog lets out a huge wail.

Earl turns to Bubba and demands, "Bubba, what's wrong with your dawg?"

Bubba says, "Well, Earl, he's sittin' on a nail."

Earl responds, "Well, Bubba, why don't he move?"

"Well, Earl," Bubba says, "I guess it don't hurt bad enough."

We're all sitting on some type of nail. Unfortunately, most of us don't hurt bad enough to get off the nail and we end up more comfortable with old problems than new solutions. If we do make a change, it's because we're so uncomfortable with the status quo that we're willing to get off the nail, or the future is so compelling that we're willing to risk discomfort in order to get there.

What's worse, we often go to extraordinary and dangerous lengths to make ourselves comfortable sitting on our nails...dulling the pain with food, alcohol, hours in front of the TV, anything to help us forget that some part of our lives isn't working and is causing us pain.

One psychological construct, called experiential avoidance, says that a lot of destructive behaviors we fall into, such as addiction, we do in order to avoid experiencing the pain in our lives. We have a painful situation, or thoughts, emotions, or circumstances, and instead of facing the pain of the situation or the pain of changing it, we just dull the pain with food, drugs, alcohol, or other things that stimulate the pleasure centers of our minds. The pleasure of eating food, for example, masks the pain of feeling bad about how things are going in our jobs, relationships, finances, or elsewhere. Of course, once the pleasure wears off, we're right back where we were. Then, depending on what we used to dull the pain, we now have new consequences.

Some people turn to food and the new consequence is a weight problem. Some turn to shopping and the new consequence is debt. Others turn to drugs, alcohol, or other unhealthy vices.

Whatever our poison, the fact is that the nail is still there and we're still sitting on it. We just did something to dull the pain for a little bit. The problem is still before us and we still have to make the decision to either go through a tough change or keep ourselves parked on the nail.

Get Off the Nail

Evan's aggression was our nail. I had done everything imaginable to avoid hospitalization—outpatient therapy, diet changes, behavior modification, a varietal cocktail of medications, Eastern medicine, and more. Taking my little boy to the hospital felt like such a drastic move. And it was facing something I didn't want to admit—how bad things were getting. There were other factors that kept me sitting on that nail. I worried that he would be scared. And frankly, I knew it would be expensive. Really expensive. But we finally arrived at a point where the pain of staying the same was greater than the pain of change.

I was distracted when working with clients, I was in tears daily, and I was constantly waiting to hear from Evan's school, only to find out that he had threatened more students or hurt more teachers. I was desperate. It was time to get off the nail.

For most of us, there literally is a tipping point where we realize that the pain we face in changing can't possibly be worse than the pain we're living with every day. At that moment, standing up and doing something new usually doesn't feel good. Those initial stages of change are very, very hard. Imagine walking around after having your butt parked on a nail for years! Ouch!

It helps, at those moments, to focus on the inspiration part of the equation. Look to your dream board, the vision of what you hope for. Focus on how much better your life will be once you go through this difficult time. Find stories, books, music, movies, that lift your sights and spirits. Hold onto that inspiration.

Slowly, healing comes. You realize that a pain you've been living with for a long time is smaller. Perhaps an old habit you've always been unhappy about is no longer pulling you. Things are getting better.

If you stay on the nail, they never do.

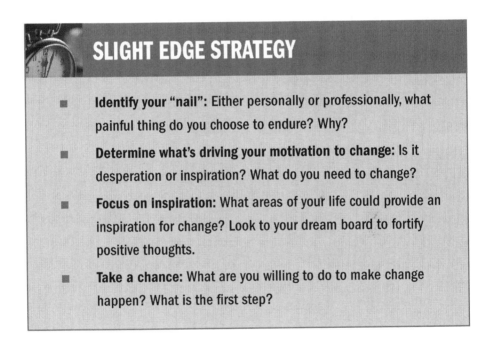

SLIGHT EDGE STRATEGY

- **Identify your "nail":** Either personally or professionally, what painful thing do you choose to endure? Why?

- **Determine what's driving your motivation to change:** Is it desperation or inspiration? What do you need to change?

- **Focus on inspiration:** What areas of your life could provide an inspiration for change? Look to your dream board to fortify positive thoughts.

- **Take a chance:** What are you willing to do to make change happen? What is the first step?

STRATEGY 9: Rethink Happiness

One day when I was talking with my mom, she looked at me, paused, and said, "Annie, are you happy?" My response was: "Mom, happiness happens in blips." She got a very confused look on her face and said, "Honey, maybe you need to start seeing a therapist…"

Here's what I meant: Most of us look at our lives and say "I am happy" or "I am not happy" based on a handful of things that are going on at the time. We tend to think of happiness as a destination. We think happiness looks like the end of a Disney cartoon where the story ends tidily and everyone lives happily ever after. Cue the lights…fade into the sunset.

That's not the way life works. We are not cartoons. And if we're lucky, our sunsets are followed by sunrises that bring all kinds of circumstances that could topple yesterday's perfect ending. Happiness is not a constant state. No one is always happy or never happy. Happiness, just like sadness and probably every other emotion, happens in little blips. Not happy with what's going on in your life? Just wait. It's a blip. Feeling angry, frustrated, or overwhelmed? Look for blips of relief and realize that this, too, shall pass. Although some blips last longer than others, everything happens in blips. Truthfully, if it weren't for the blips, we wouldn't recognize happiness at all. Happiness is only happiness because we also have times of stress, anxiety, sadness, loneliness, and boredom. In order to even recognize and experience happiness, we need to have not-so-happy times to compare it with. How do we know when we're eating amazing food? Because we've had some *really* crappy food!

The Choice Is Yours

A great deal of the way we experience happiness depends on which blips we choose to focus on. I know people who, as soon as they feel happy, start waiting for the other shoe to drop. They don't focus on the happy blip; they have their eyes peeled for the next disappointment.

My mom's question inspired me to think about where I was with respect to happiness. Evan was in a good place. He was eight-and-a-half years old and a year had passed since our life-altering stint at the hospital. My business had taken off. I had a beautiful happy, healthy 10-year-old daughter, Rylee, and I was married to a man that I was (and still am) madly in love with.

That said, I still had two large claw marks scratched in my back that were stinging and painful. Evan didn't make them out of rage like he'd done so many times before. In fact, his aggression had gone way down, exactly as I had envisioned on my dream board.

With frontal lobe deficits, severe ADHD, mood swings, and a very difficult time processing, organizing, and managing all of the stimuli that come his way, he was still dealing with a great deal of hyperactivity, impulsiveness, and mania. He made the scratches in an attempt to give me a hug. Although things were a lot better, I still got angry, frustrated, and sometimes lost my cool.

Am I happy with my life? Absolutely. Am I stressed, overwhelmed, neurotic, and anxious sometimes? Absolutely. Both can be true, and it can change from one to another in a matter of moments.

Although I could cite things I was very happy about—my marriage, Evan's improvement, my thriving business—I still had to *decide* to be happy. I had to choose to focus on those happy blips instead of the more difficult ones that were still there, like having a child who was still very ill.

Destination Happiness?

Our destination version of happiness usually relies on this sentence: "If_____, then I will be happy." *If I fall in love. If I have a different job. If I live in a different house. If I have more money. If I have better health.* The list goes on and on. What do we have to get in order to be happy?

If happiness is about circumstances, then you're at the mercy of everything. Anything you can get to make you happy, you can un-get. And usually, even when you get what you want, you have to *remember* to be happy about it. Think of what you wanted 10 years ago. Chances are, you've done it, been there, or now have it, and you may still be unhappy.

Scientists have studied groups of people a decade after a pivotal event. In one study, one group had won the lottery; the other group had become paraplegics through illness or injury. It's obvious who is happier, right? Wrong. Research shows that a year after winning the lottery and a year after someone loses the use of their limbs, both groups actually rated themselves at the same level of happiness.[6]

In order to be a happy person, we don't need to *get* anything. We need to change our perspective on happiness. Happiness isn't a feeling, it's a habit that you cultivate. The feeling of happiness ebbs and flows, but a habit is something you choose and act toward.

How? That's what we'll tackle in the next strategy.

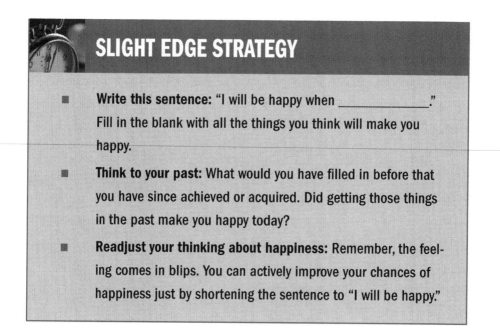

SLIGHT EDGE STRATEGY

- **Write this sentence:** "I will be happy when _____." Fill in the blank with all the things you think will make you happy.

- **Think to your past:** What would you have filled in before that you have since achieved or acquired. Did getting those things in the past make you happy today?

- **Readjust your thinking about happiness:** Remember, the feeling comes in blips. You can actively improve your chances of happiness just by shortening the sentence to "I will be happy."

---

[6]Shawn Achor, *The Happiness Advantage: The Seven Principles of Positive Psychology That Fuel Success and Performance at Work* (New York: Crown Business, 2010).

STRATEGY 10:
Adopt the Happiness Habit

I n his book, *The Happiness Advantage*,[7] Shawn Achor explains that 90 percent of long-term happiness is based on the way our brain processes the world. Achor explains that if we can raise our level of positivity in the present, our brains experience a happiness advantage. Your brain, in a positive state, is more than 30 percent more productive, creative, and intelligent than it is when it is negative or stressed.

Consequently, we make better decisions, find more feasible solutions, and enjoy the whole process more when we're happy. And that makes us even happier.

You're probably thinking, "Yeah, that's nice, but how do I do it? How do I become happy?" As I discussed in Strategy 9, the first step is to make the choice. You have to decide to work toward happiness.

As a culture, we've been locked for a long time in a kind of hopeless naval-gazing. We've gotten in the habit, partially thanks to modern psychology, of focusing on what is *wrong* in our lives in order to fix it and make it *right*. And yet our level of depression has continued to grow. Countering that trend, many psychologists have shifted their emphasis from constantly picking through the ruins to looking for what is positive and possible, according to an article called "The Science of Happiness."[8] Although dealing with issues realistically is still important, research has shown remarkable success from strength-based, positive psychology.

Genetics and hard wiring aside, we have direct control over much of our happiness. That means even if we have a screwed up family (who

---

[7]Ibid.

[8]Craig Lambert, "The Science of Happiness," *The Harvard Magazine* (January–February 2007), available at http://harvardmagazine.com/2007/01/the-science-of-happiness.html.

doesn't?) and have endured our share of hardships (who hasn't?), we still have the ability to control our own happiness. That's huge! It has been scientifically proven that we can generate our own happiness, regardless of our situation and circumstances.

Happiness isn't a one and done. Remember, it's not a constant state—it's a blip. You have to keep working toward happiness the same way you keep working toward a healthier body, or a cleaner house, or a better career.

Just like with those things, there are practical steps you can take toward becoming happier:

- **Take care of your body:** In her book *The Happiness Project*,[9] Gretchen Rubin says sleep is the new sex. Adults need a substantial amount of sleep every night. We are currently getting an average of 6.9 hours during the week and 7.9 on the weekends, 20 percent less than we did 100 years ago. Although we try to adjust to feeling sleepy, lack of sleep impairs our memory, weakens our immune system, slows our metabolism, and just makes us cranky. Want to be happier? Get more sleep. Just be careful not to use sleep as an escape. Too much of anything is not a good thing.

- **Foster relationships:** In all of the research, the number one determinant of happiness continues to be our relationships with others. Spending time with people we care about, engaging in activities we enjoy, and thinking about positive things may actually seem like work at times, but the payoff is invaluable.

- **Cultivate gratitude:** Start a gratitude journal. Every day, write down a handful of things you feel grateful for. Focusing on these blips fosters happiness.

---

[9]Gretchen Rubin, *The Happiness Project: Or, Why I Spent a Year Trying to Sing in the Morning, Clean My Closets, Fight Right, Read Aristotle, and Generally Have More Fun* (New York: HarperCollins, 2009).

- **Make happiness a priority:** Make time for what is important to you. It's easy to get bogged down in life, only to realize 10 years have slipped by. Make happiness something you work on every day.

- **Practice happiness:** Practice makes perfect. Find small things to be happy about each day and enjoy them! I love to catch myself dancing and singing in my car to a great song. (Try this while waiting at a red light. If you don't get happy doing it, at least the people around you will get a good laugh!)

- **Take a risk!** We all end up in a rut at times. Just be careful not to stay there too long. Life is short. Live it!

- **Stop waiting:** Forget the "I'll be happy when..." or you'll waste your life waiting for that happy moment to come. You will never have the "perfect" life. It doesn't exist. Enjoy the now. Look for and enjoy those perfect moments—or attempt to find the humor in the imperfect ones.

When we were in crisis mode before Evan was hospitalized, we would watch funny movies and listen to comedians regularly. It helped so much that I made it a habit to watch funny movies and shows and avoid those that brought me down. We find what we look for, so look for funny!

And remember Slight Edge changes. A little goes a long way. Every single day, regardless of how crappy you might feel, find something to be happy about. Even if you only find one thing each day, that's 365 happy things a year! It's the little things done consistently that make the biggest impact.

SLIGHT EDGE STRATEGY

- **Choose happiness:** Build a new habit of happiness one day at a time. Start small. Pick one thought or behavior a day and cultivate your thoughts toward being happy about that one small thing. When you have that one down, find another.

- **Cultivate the habit of happiness:** Share examples, stories, and small things that bring a smile to your face with the people in your life. Happiness is contagious! You'll find that once you begin to focus on these moments, there become many more of them.

STRATEGY 11: Focus on Gratitude

Feeling gratitude and not expressing it is like wrapping a present and not giving it.—William Arthur Ward

Be grateful. It's such a simple statement, yet so powerful, that it has completely changed my life. I had been missing something that was right in front of me the whole time: gratitude. How much time do we spend complaining—in our thoughts or in our words or actions—about what we have, don't have, want, can't get, or get too much of? I know for me, it was entirely too much. We only have a certain amount of physical and emotional energy to spend each day. How much of it are you wasting on negative thoughts, people, and circumstances?

A lot of us grew up being told: "Eat your vegetables! Kids wish they had those vegetables in (some underdeveloped country)." And we always thought (or at least I did), "Well, they can have mine."

Sometimes, being told to be grateful feels like that. When you think about it, we can get so focused on the nicer house we don't have, the better job, the higher salary, and so forth, that we forget that 80 percent of the world lives on less than $10 a day. In many countries, people forfeit their lives for sharing their opinions. In others, children die from diarrhea, malaria, and other diseases we would treat easily. We forget—because we have real struggles, chronic pain, unemployment, or difficult relationships—that there are many, many things to be grateful for.

The Secret's Out

The Secret[10] started as a book and evolved into a movement: everything is possible, nothing is impossible. The philosophy is that we create our own reality, and that if we want a great one, we first have to appreciate what we have.

---

[10]Rhonda Byrne, *The Secret* (New York: First Atria Books, 2006).

I really struggled with this concept at one point in my life. What did I have to be grateful for? My kiddo was sick, I was a single mom, and I was miserable. It took some soul searching, but I realized how fortunate I was. I had friends, my mother had moved next door to help take care of Evan, I had an incredible day care provider, and I had what so many moms in my situation don't have: a support system.

I had joined NAMI, and started taking classes. I met incredible parents who had children in similar situations, and it made all the difference. Finally someone got where I was coming from and didn't blame me.

As soon as I started becoming truly grateful for all of the blessings and gifts in my life, it was like a switch turned on and amazing things started to happen. I met my husband, Jay, a man who I am convinced should wear a cape, and his beautiful daughter, Rylee. We found yet another amazing caregiver, and we began getting support from multiple doctors. I credit all of those things with gratitude.

Are you struggling to find things to be grateful for? Try these strategies to shift your focus to one of gratitude:

1. **Keep a gratitude journal:** Each day when you wake up, write down a few of the things you are grateful for. It might be that you had a bed to sleep in or air conditioning to keep you cool. It could be that you got to wake up! When you go to sleep, write down a few of the things you are grateful for that happened during your day. Try to really think about your day and be specific.

2. **Say "thank you" at every opportunity:** If someone holds a door for you or does something nice, rather than the quick nod of the head, turn to them and with sincerity, say "thank you."

3. **Appreciate the little things:** Make a list of the little things that are important to you and can make a difference in your mood. Whether it is drinking coffee from your favorite cup or reading before you go to sleep, find ways to incorporate these into your daily routine and stop to appreciate them when they happen.

4. **Let the people you care about know they are important to you:**
    Whether it's a quick email, a sticky note, or a hug, something so
    simple makes all the difference. Make it a goal to reach out to one
    or two people each week. Maintaining relationships takes work,
    but the rewards are endless.

5. **Erase "but" from your vocabulary:** It's easy to say, I'm grateful for
    these clothes, but I sure would like new ones. Or, I'm blessed to
    have my family, but they sure are crazy. (Lord knows this applies to
    most of us!) Our mind doesn't hear the word "but"; it just hears "I
    want new clothes" or "my family is crazy." "But" negates everything
    that precedes it. While it might seem insignificant, this is a big
    step that most people miss. We believe what we tell ourselves, and
    what we think about, we bring about.

SLIGHT EDGE STRATEGY

- **Start a gratitude journal:** Reflect on your day each evening
  and write a few things that you are thankful or grateful for. Did
  you sail through a green light? Find $5 in your pocket? Giggle
  at someone who passed gas in an elevator? Even the smallest
  moments can create happiness.

- **Be grateful:** What are you grateful for right now? Once being
  grateful becomes a habit, you'll be amazed at how many
  things you'll find to be thankful for.

- **Be kind:** Reach out to the people in your life whom you value
  and love. Maintain your relationships.

STRATEGY 12: Live from Your Core

Every day, we make hundreds of decisions, have thousands of thoughts, and spend much of our time responding and reacting to other people and circumstances. Without even realizing it, we sometimes neglect that solid place within us where we hold our true beliefs and values. I call this place our core. If we want to live from our core, we have to be clear about these beliefs because they guide most of our decisions. Should you go to your friend's birthday party when you'd rather stay at home? Do you turn the work project in late because you had other things going on? Should you honk at the car that just cut you off? Your answers depend on your core beliefs.

Write down these central, fundamental beliefs and make choices based on them. That way, we're not frenetically responding to the onslaught of information thrown at us 24/7. Our actions and words come from our most deeply held beliefs about who we are and who we want to be.

I must have written down my core beliefs and values at some time, but I don't remember, and I don't know if time and circumstances have altered them. So I went through the exercise again. Turns out, it's a little challenging. You can't just whip out a belief that you hold in the deepest part of yourself. You have to think: What do I want to be my driving motivations for the way I live my life?

Here are some of mine:

■ I believe in finding joy in life, whether it's a good laugh with a friend or taking my dog for a walk.

- I believe that I am responsible for my choices and actions, and that I have the power to choose how I handle my life. I'm responsible for my own happiness.

- I believe that I have the power to affect others' lives—for the better or the worse—and I choose the former in the way I live.

- I believe that the people who are most important to me—like family and friends—should get the best I have to offer.

- I believe that I can find and hold onto the good in myself and help other people find and be inspired by the good in themselves.

- I believe I should be gentle with myself, give myself a break, and give myself time to learn, change, and grow without beating myself up.

Reflecting on what I truly believe, I can see there are many days when I don't live from my core. My family frequently gets the worst of me, and I reserve the best parts of me for clients or friends. Of course, I promptly beat myself up, and seriously, the gloves are off!

We spend so much time responding to the demands of the moment, that day by day we can slip into becoming a different person than we intended, living a life that seems to be of someone else's design. We don't like the way it makes us feel, or the work we do, or the relationships we have with others. We're not sure how we got here…or how to get out.

When we write down our core beliefs and values and make those the guiding principles for how we handle everything, from interactions with family and colleagues to how we handle traffic or spend our leisure time, we find ourselves living in a way that feels right. It's a form of integrity in which what we believe and what we say and what we do all line up.

I can give myself permission to take time to do something that's fun, because it aligns with my core values to find the joy in life.

When Evan's being a challenge, or I encounter someone who is being difficult or unreasonable, I can choose to respond to that person with patience, honesty, and respect. And I'm not doing it because they deserve it or I'm afraid to do otherwise; I'm doing it because, in my core, that's how I believe in treating people. I'm not responding to that person's problems; I'm living from my core beliefs and values.

And when I inevitably fail—and make no mistake, I do—I can treat myself as I would a friend, with gentleness and patience. Because that's one of my core values, too.

Owning your core brings this great sense of peace, and you're making choices because of what you believe instead of reacting to other people and situations.

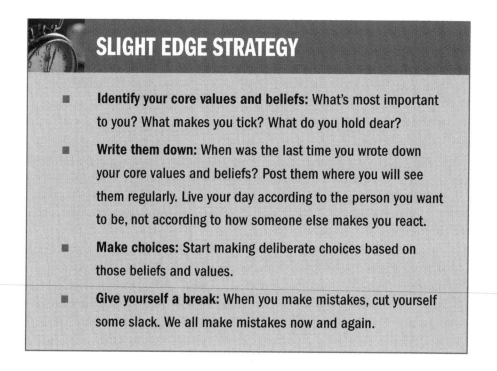

SLIGHT EDGE STRATEGY

- **Identify your core values and beliefs:** What's most important to you? What makes you tick? What do you hold dear?

- **Write them down:** When was the last time you wrote down your core values and beliefs? Post them where you will see them regularly. Live your day according to the person you want to be, not according to how someone else makes you react.

- **Make choices:** Start making deliberate choices based on those beliefs and values.

- **Give yourself a break:** When you make mistakes, cut yourself some slack. We all make mistakes now and again.

STRATEGY 13:
Remove the Boxing Gloves

've spent a lot of time "shoulding" myself: *I should have...I could have...I wish I would have...*

While it's completely normal to beat ourselves up a little when we make a mistake, too many times we go for a total knockout. When we start down that path, we allow ourselves to accumulate and dwell upon negative messages that are completely self-defeating. We inadvertently sabotage our own success.

Shelf Self-Doubt

One day when Evan was five years old, we were in Walmart shopping. He got angry because I wouldn't buy him his tenth basketball, called me a bitch, and knocked down an end cap display. Some woman looked at me, rolled her eyes, and said, "Maybe if you smacked his ass once in a while, he wouldn't act like that!"

After my initial shock of both Evan's and that lady's behavior, and while fighting back tears, I started doubting every ounce of my ability as a mother. The truth is, I had tried spanking him, and it only made matters a hundred times worse. He would get incredibly violent, and I was inadvertently teaching him to be aggressive by being aggressive myself.

I was trying every possible strategy, and Evan was still out of control. I constantly felt like a failure. After lots of therapy and plenty of my own medication, I realized I had to start giving myself a break. I was doing the best I could, given my situation, as are most of us. I started looking at both myself and other people more kindly, with more generosity, with more patience. And that took an enormous weight from me.

Next time you're tempted to go to blows with yourself, stop. Give yourself a time-out. Grant yourself permission to look over the situation, what actions you took, or choices you made. Consider what you could do differently next time. *Then let it go!*

Ruminating on it won't change anything; it will only make you feel worse.

We're human. We're flawed and imperfect beings. We screw up. But guess what? The sun will still come up tomorrow. Treat yourself the same way you would treat a friend who made the same mistake: Gently, and with a lot of understanding and forgiveness. Take off your boxing gloves and give yourself a break!

Whether you are beating yourself up over a bad decision or standing in the way of your own success, here are some things you can do to get out of your own way:

1. **Ignore the negative things you say to yourself:** We send ourselves negative messages that are completely self-defeating. Attitudes can only be formed, fed, and nurtured by suggestions in our minds and the words that come out of our mouths. We've spent a long time with these old messages. It's going to take time to adopt some new ones. We must be diligent about shutting down negative thoughts and be deliberate about what we say to ourselves.

2. **Stop striving to be mediocre:** It's so easy to get wrapped up trying to "fix" our weaknesses, and the result is that we end up with mediocrity. If you're introverted, you might have a desire to be more social; if you're extroverted, maybe you want to be more introspective. Find the things you do well, that come naturally to you, and focus on those!

3. **Keep it small:** Rather than breaking your back—and your spirit—by trying to accomplish everything at once, focus on making subtle changes, consistently. Once you master those, move on to others. When we try to do everything at once, we defeat ourselves before we even get started.

4. **Get help:** If you're spinning your wheels and unable or unwilling to help yourself, enlist a trusted a friend or loved one to give you a push. While we all like friends who are sweet and loving, we also need the ones who don't blow smoke at us and will hold us to our own best expectations. Just don't limit yourself to your BFFs (Best Friends Forever). Try to find BBFs (Business Best Friends) and friends who enjoy similar interests.

5. **Challenge yourself:** While you certainly don't want to set yourself up for failure by setting unrealistic goals, you also need to stretch yourself and get out of your comfort zone.

6. **Lighten up!** I don't know how or when, but we have gotten so uptight and serious. Next time you get in an elevator, watch how all of the people just stare straight ahead or at the ascending or descending floor numbers to avoid conversation. Certainly there are days I do the same, but sometimes I'll burst out with a joke: "Two guys walk into a bar. The third one ducks." People can't help but smile, and smiling is contagious.

SLIGHT EDGE STRATEGY

■ **Be your own BFF:** Switch from being your own harshest critic to your own best friend. Pay attention to how you respond to mistakes. Quit beating yourself up. What encouraging words would you say to someone else who made that mistake? Say them to yourself.

■ **Lighten up:** Each day, remember to take it easy on yourself. Make the choice not to beat yourself up.

STRATEGY 14:
Embrace Everyday Miracles

A man is sitting on his porch as floodwaters rise. A woman floats by in a boat and asks if the man needs help. "No, thank you," says the man, "I'm trusting in the Lord."

The waters rise higher, sending the man upstairs. A raft full of people floats by his second story window. "Get in, there's plenty of room," they say. "No thanks," says the man, "I'm trusting in the Lord."

The floodwaters keep rising, forcing the man up to the roof. A helicopter swoops in, lowering its ladder for the man. "Thanks anyway," shouts the man, "I'm trusting in the Lord." Finally, the man is swept away in the torrent and drowns.

At the gates of Heaven, the man asks God, "Why didn't you save me?"

"What do you mean?" replies God, "I sent two boats and a helicopter."

When I first heard this story, I laughed hard, recognizing myself. I could relate to the man on the porch. Evan's violent and strange behavior had been escalating for years, and we had run into one doctor after another who said, "The best thing you can do is hospitalize him." I had such an aversion to the idea, though, that I kept looking for another doctor to give me a different solution. I tried and tried until I wore out my hope, my energy, and my resources.

Finally, I gave up and we took Evan to the hospital. Guess what? That was exactly what we needed. It's funny how we can get fixated on—or against—a particular solution to our problems or challenges. We don't want to be told we have to exercise and eat differently; we just want medication to bring down our blood pressure or make us thinner. We don't want to learn to assert ourselves; we just want the boss to recognize our value and give us a raise. We don't want to learn a new way of handling conflict with our spouse; we just want him or her to realize we're right!

In the case of the man on the roof, he expected God to operate in some miraculous way, and he couldn't even see or be grateful when God sent pretty mundane—but still life-saving—solutions. And frequently, that's the way it works. If you can't find your car keys, you might get divine intervention, but cleaning up the clutter and creating a spot for the keys works well, too. If you're late to the meeting, again, you might get all the traffic lights to go green at just the right moment, or you might leave the house 15 minutes earlier so you can be on time.

Other times—and this can be even more frustrating—the answer lies in the thing we least wanted to happen, like when we took Evan to the hospital.

I had built up in my mind the idea that leaving my baby in a psychiatric hospital with a bunch of strangers was the worst thing in the world. So I wore myself out avoiding it. I had visions of Evan being terrified, of him having all kinds of horrible treatments, and being stigmatized for the rest of his life—as if he got some sort of hospital tattoo on his forehead.

As it turned out, yes, he was scared for a bit. Then he got over it. He was surrounded by people who had an understanding of him and what he was going through—for the first time in his life. And we were given some clarity and peace of mind, as well as some tools and strategies to better help him and manage his behavior. Not at all the horrible scenario I envisioned.

Let's face it, for most people, losing their jobs, getting divorced, losing their homes, or being diagnosed with a major illness doesn't look like an answer to anything. It just looks like a tragedy. Yet, a year or so later, many people will say that losing their job was the catalyst they needed to finding a career they really loved. Discovering a medical condition spurred them to create a happier, healthier life. The end of the marriage was the beginning of finding their strengths and dreams.

The solution is to have your eyes, heart, and mind open for unexpected answers to the things you struggle with. Be prepared for solutions to come from the least expected places. And, when you can, try to find the bright spots and answers that come in packages you didn't want at all.

This is especially difficult and important when the solution to your problem is changing *you*, rather than changing others around you or changing your circumstances. The good news is that you have a lot more power to change yourself and the way you relate to the world than you do over anything else. So in a way, the solution to dealing with a sometimes tumultuous world is to gain better control over your own thoughts and attitudes.

While it's not the rescue from the others' behavior that most of us are looking for, it is a good, solid boat to help us ride out the floodwaters.

SLIGHT EDGE STRATEGY

- **Ask questions:** What answers or solutions have you been seeking? Where could you look for these answers?

- **Look for the obvious solutions:** What "boats and helicopters" have been coming your way that you may have been ignoring?

- **Open yourself to new solutions:** What will be your strategy the next time you're given an unexpected solution? How will you identify it?

STRATEGY 15: Build Resilience

Lately, I really have come to appreciate the concept of resilience. Resilience is defined as the ability to recover from, or adjust easily to, misfortune or change. I have been thinking about resilience partly because of my own life and partly because I watch the news. You can't watch for too long without hearing about horrible tragedies, people who have lost everything in a flood or hurricane, or someone who is hanging on for dear life because they were a victim of senseless violence. When traumatic things happen, how do you recover?

Every day people lose jobs or loved ones, get diagnosed with illnesses, and suffer unspeakable tragedies. How do we bounce back? What does resilience look like?

When we first go through something horrible, it seems we'll never be able to bounce back. We are overwhelmed with grief, fear, or some other emotion. Slowly it dawns on us that there's no going back. We must find the strength and the will to go forward. We may not be able to make big strides at first, but we begin taking small steps to work toward a solution and to find ways to carry on.

When the chips are down—and you're down with them—how do you get back up? Here are a few strategies that will help build resilience.

1. **Keep the big picture in mind:** This may feel like the only moment in your life that matters. Chances are, you've felt that way before. Do you remember? It is incredibly easy to lose sight of the forest and get stuck in the trees when you are knocked down. Focus on what is truly important and only on things you can directly affect.

2. **Focus on your strengths and accomplishments:** When you're knocked down, it's easy to feel down. Remember what makes you

amazing. You are full of strengths, accomplishments, and good-ness. You are strong and capable of handling anything that is thrown your way. You have done it before and you will do it again.

3. **Take care of yourself:** Many of us have learned to put other people's needs before our own. And in a difficult time, when you need it the most, it's easy to forget to take care of yourself. Make a concerted effort to eat right, exercise, take time alone, read a positive and uplifting book, and just be kind to yourself. You need these things to keep up your strength, emotionally and physically, to deal with your circumstances. Take time for yourself. You will never *find* this time. You have to *make* this time.

4. **Take a moment to feel what you feel:** In the effort to move forward, sometimes we forget to give ourselves time to feel what we're feeling—whether it's grief, disappointment, or sadness. Give yourself permission to stop and pay attention to how you're feeling. Have that good cry if you need it. Many times we try to "stuff" those feelings, and this causes them to manifest in many different ways—headaches, illness, weight loss or gain, etc. It's okay to feel what you feel. Just remember not to get stuck there.

5. **Focus on what you can control:** Rather than getting wrapped up in what ifs, other people's faults, or external events, focus on the things over which you have direct and immediate control. What can you do today, right now, to make things better or different?

6. **Surround yourself with positive people:** A support system is one of the biggest tools in your arsenal. Surround yourself with people who are loving, kind, supportive, and positive. Sometimes when we go through tough times we don't want to burden people. You probably know the people who will feel burdened and the ones who would be happy to have an opportunity to lift your spirits. Go for the latter.

7. **Look back:** Look back on times when you felt like life had knocked you down and you couldn't imagine getting back up, laughing, or thinking of lighthearted things like picnics or road trips. It seemed like nothing would ever be good again. And then it was. And it will be again.

8. **Reframe the way you're thinking:** Hard things have a way of teaching us the lessons that wind up changing our lives the most, for the better. What can you learn from this experience? How can this make you stronger? How can this prepare you for the struggles you will surely continue to experience in your life? What little lessons can you eke out of the situation?

If you've been knocked down lately, focus on resilience. I have to keep reminding myself that I would not be given more than I am capable of handling. We are resilient by nature; we just have to work a little harder at it some days. And remember, as you come through this, you will one day be the person helping someone else get through a really hard time, holding out hope that things can get better.

SLIGHT EDGE STRATEGY

- **Be proactive:** Before a situation arises, make a list of strategies that can help you be more resilient. Don't wait until crisis to figure out ways to cope more effectively. When the going gets tough, what are 10–15 things that you can do build resilience?

- **Keep getting up:** Think about a time when you were knocked down. What lesson can you take from that experience? What did you learn? How can you use that knowledge the next time you are struggling?

STRATEGY 16: Rock What You Have

I love that the secret's out about Photoshopping models and actresses. It's very comforting to know that a lot of computer enhancements go into making these women look flawless. We increasingly see pictures of famous people as they appear before they're "redone." It's almost as if they're real people like us.

Are they still beautiful without the heavy makeup and the artificial shaping of their bodies? Yes, but they're regular-person beautiful, not other-worldly person beautiful. They have regular bodies with parts they no doubt wish they could change. They look like somebody I could have coffee with.

So many people tend to see these "perfect" models and actresses and compare themselves to the images. And this comparison is rarely positive. And that's only one area where we compare ourselves. We all have a tendency to compare ourselves to other people. There's always someone who has a nicer or cleaner house, a flashier car, or a better job. They are natural leaders, contribute to more causes, eat healthier, exercise more, have more friends, throw more parties, make more money, are better traveled, or have a happier marriage. If it's another parent, they spend more quality time with their kids, have more successful kids, or participate in more school events.

There are, in fact, thousands of ways to be and thousands of things to be good at. We can only manage to excel at a few things—and so can everybody else! When we're in a certain frame of mind, we compare ourselves to others who have some quality we admire or possession we covet. Guess who comes up short? When we do this, it's easy to completely forget what it is that makes us special and unique.

Nobody is good at everything. Some people do a lot of crafts with their kids. I certainly try, but it's just not my thing. Yet when I see a mom who has spent the afternoon making cookies in the shape of robots and frosting them for a kid's birthday party, I often forget all the things I bring to my own family—my sense of humor, my integrity, my love, my tenacity—and I then realize that those are admirable traits as well. So what if I can't make robot cookies? I spend quality time with my kids, and I truly love them.

If I had a friend who made that same comparison about herself and someone else, I would leap to her defense and tell her about all the admirable characteristics I thought she had. Isn't it strange, though, that we rarely do that for ourselves?

When we compare ourselves to other people, we are more self-critical. We don't have the advantages, skills, or talents that other person was given. We have our own. And we don't know what struggles or weaknesses that other person wrestles with every day. We have only our own. Whatever we want to change about ourselves is under our control. Whatever we have today, we have to learn to rock it!

Rock that sense of humor or that analytical mind. Enjoy it and make the most out of it. Celebrate that kind heart or that ability to organize things almost instinctively. Work that passion for your social cause, your tendency to rescue puppies, or your gift of bringing food to struggling families who need it.

Rock what you've got! It is physically, mentally, and emotionally exhausting and taxing to try to keep up with an image of what you think the "perfect" mother, father, employee, boss, or friend should look like.

Stop comparing yourself to others and start embracing who you are and what you have to offer. Quit keeping up with the Joneses. Here's to you, Mrs. Jones:

Dear Mrs. Jones,

I am exhausted trying to keep up with you. I hereby pledge to no longer secretly mentally compete with you. For my own mental health, I will no longer attempt to live by your standards. I refuse to be defeated by continually comparing myself to who you are, what you do, and what you have. I am in my own right a beautiful, successful, talented, and loving person. I am happy with who I am today.

Sincerely,

Anne

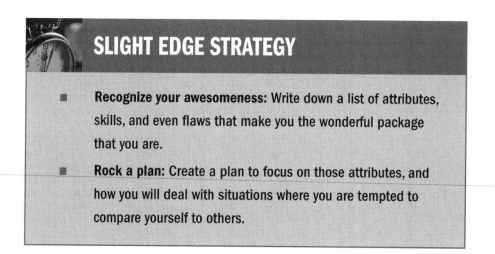

SLIGHT EDGE STRATEGY

- **Recognize your awesomeness:** Write down a list of attributes, skills, and even flaws that make you the wonderful package that you are.

- **Rock a plan:** Create a plan to focus on those attributes, and how you will deal with situations where you are tempted to compare yourself to others.

STRATEGY 17: Ignore Negative Voices

Jill Bolte Taylor is a brain scientist who had a stroke. The left side of her brain—the side that analyzes, categorizes, and makes sense of experiences—was flooded with blood and essentially shut down. The right side—the side that experiences things without judgment—took over. And what she found was bliss. She kept melting into a vast universe where she felt connected to everything.

When she recovered, she wrote a book called *My Stroke of Insight*,[11] which detailed her experiences of trying to keep hold of that bliss even when her inner analyzer returned.

We all have an inner analyzer in our left brain that talks all day long. It tells us useful things, like our name and address, how to drive a car, and how to do our jobs. It helps us make decisions and use our debit card at the grocery store.

It also says a bunch of other useless crap. It might tell us that the strange look our boss just gave us means we're about to get fired. And not only are we going to get fired, we'll never find another job in this economy. And then we won't be able to afford our house, our kids will have to change schools, and on and on.

Sometimes it tells us nice things. It tells us that the good conversation we had with the client means we're going to land the project, which means we'll probably get a raise and maybe even a promotion. It tells us that we are intelligent, have integrity, and make a difference.

This brain chatter is intertwined with the information we need to carry out simple tasks. This chatter creates stories in our heads that pull us out of the reality of the moment and into some world in our own mind. In reality, our boss gave us a funny look and we don't know why. It might be

---

[11] Jill Bolte Taylor, *My Stroke of Insight: A Brain Scientist's Personal Journey* (New York: Penguin Books, 2006).

indigestion. But our left brain starts building stories around it—even stories that aren't nice and are not what's really happening.

Often it's totally subconscious. We might be near the end of the story before we realize we were spinning a story at all.

Not all brain chatter is bad. I have a voice that's very wise and empathic; I call her the angel on my shoulder. She reminds me of my goals and priorities and encourages me to be brave and make good choices. However, on my other shoulder, I have a little devil who can cause the good, angelic side to doubt herself. When I feel rested and my life seems in order, the angel wins. But when I'm tired or feeling over-whelmed, my little devil takes the prize.

I may go out to eat with every intention of having a salad. Then the little devil starts spinning a story, which I know isn't true, about how the cheeseburger and fries *really* aren't that bad—after all, I need the protein after such a really bad day! As I stare at the remaining few fry bits that are left on my plate, that rotten, negative little voice contemptuously says: "Great, now you're going to gain five pounds."

When the little angel tells us that we are totally capable and should jump at the exciting new opportunity at work, our little devil says it's too overwhelming, and we already have enough on our plate. If our angel is so wise, and our devil is so incredibly malevolent, why do we spend so much time listening to the negative? How do we tune it out?

For one thing, heeding our devil requires very little work. Obeying it usually takes us down the path of least resistance. It's so familiar and easy, we don't even realize we're sliding down the slippery slope. Whether it's the internal debate to bite our tongue when we want to make an unproductive comment, or that nagging voice that tells us we're not smart enough, it's time to reign in that little imp.

I've found it to be helpful to make a mental image of my devil (I see Homer Simpson with horns. My angel is an adorable puppy…or Bradley Cooper). It helps to be able to shut "it" down if you know what "it" looks like. Then start really listening for that voice. Sometimes you can tell because you suddenly feel anxious or reckless or some other feeling that you don't associate with positive behaviors. Frequently, in the beginning, you just need to check in with yourself. Is your mind focused on what you're doing, or is it spinning a story?

Pay attention to how much more the negative creeps up when you're tired or stressed. This is when you are most vulnerable.

Once you've gotten to recognize the negative voice, try tuning it out. You won't be able to stop the chatter, but when you acknowledge it as chatter, you can let it hum in the background without it affecting your decisions, giving the angel a much better chance to steer you in the right direction.

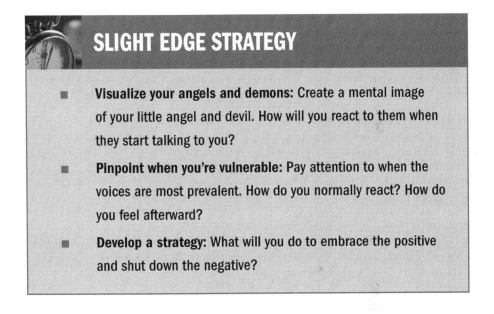

SLIGHT EDGE STRATEGY

- **Visualize your angels and demons:** Create a mental image of your little angel and devil. How will you react to them when they start talking to you?

- **Pinpoint when you're vulnerable:** Pay attention to when the voices are most prevalent. How do you normally react? How do you feel afterward?

- **Develop a strategy:** What will you do to embrace the positive and shut down the negative?

STRATEGY 18: Stop Renting

What do you do differently in a hotel room than you would in your own home? (Get your mind out of the gutter!) If you're like most people, you probably keep the room nice and cool, leave the lights on, leave the bed unmade, and maybe even leave the towels on the floor. Why would you do those things in a hotel but not in your own home? Ownership, pure and simple.

Have you ever wondered why some people walk by a piece of trash and don't pick it up? Or why others seem to give the bare minimum at work when you know they are capable of so much more? It's for much the same reason.

When we own something, we tend to take better care of it. When it is ours, we want to make sure we treat it right. In your personal and professional life, do you rent or own? Do you take ownership of relationships, projects, problems, and solutions? Do you own the choices you make each day? I know on a good day, I take complete ownership. On a bad day, it's just easier to rent.

What does it mean to take ownership of your life? It means you stop blaming other people and own what happens in your life. Maybe your boss is a poor manager and plays favorites. So you take ownership of the fact that you're deciding to remain in a job where you know your progress is blocked or accept that you may not have been aggressive enough in pursuing another position. Maybe you haven't sought out a particular certification or skill set that would make it easier to transition into another job. In each case, you're not a victim. You're making a decision to get up every morning and go to work in this job.

Perhaps you're in an unsatisfying relationship. Instead of always blaming the other person for being a so-and-so, you acknowledge that you chose this relationship, and you play some part in the way it's going. Whether that's not expressing your needs, not changing things about yourself that are creating tension in the relationship, or not leaving the relationship, you are making choices. You own your part.

In my situation with Evan, for a time, I wallowed in self-pity. Why was my child so difficult? It just wasn't fair! Why me? However, I chose to have a child, which is always a risk. And I chose to care for him myself rather than send him someplace else to live. I chose to take it as my responsibility to raise Evan to be as healthy and happy as he could be. And I know that, in some way or another, I may always be caring for Evan. Although that makes some days hard, there's real peace in having claimed ownership of that choice.

If you own something, you authorize yourself to take control of it. You immediately change from being a victim to being in the driver's seat. Many people tend to say "But I can't make that change because…" Inaction is still a choice. It's not:

- *I can't switch jobs because I can't earn this much anywhere else.* It's *I choose to stay in this job because I earn more here than I could someplace else.*

- *I can't work out because I'm already working 18 hours a day.* It's *I choose not to make working out a priority.*

When I catch my kids doing something they shouldn't be doing and I call them on it, their first reaction is to get defensive, blame someone else, or make excuses. I was working with a client who described her coworkers the same way. When I asked if she was taking ownership of the situation, her response was, "Why should I have to? They don't!"

What she didn't understand is that when she identified herself as the victim, she gave her personal power to someone else and it wouldn't be there when she needed it. It's too easy to choose the path of least resistance rather than charting your own course. The only way you're going to reach your goals is to own your journey.

I realize this can come across as insensitive and abrupt. At some point, though, we have to take ownership of our lives. We are the only ones we can control, and by giving others the power to control our destiny, we become the victim. We are responsible for our life and our happiness. You always have a choice. It might not be the choice you want, but you always have a choice.

SLIGHT EDGE STRATEGY

- **Take ownership:** Identify a situation in your life where you feel like a victim. Now, authorize yourself to take control of the situation.

- **Empower yourself:** Turn that situation around so you're not a victim. What choices are you making that allow the situation to remain the same? Why are you making those choices? What choices could you make to change the situation?

STRATEGY 19:
Be Kinder Than Necessary

I was at the grocery store in the checkout line when the woman in front of me was all but screaming at the poor bagger because he had squished her bread. My first thought was how rude she was. But then she started to cry. I'm not sure what was going on in her life, but it was obvious she was having an extremely hard time.

Sometimes, it's just tough to keep your composure when you're hanging on by a thread. I wish I could say that I've handled all of my struggles with grace and poise, but truth be told, I've been that woman in the checkout line. I've snapped at people and have not been the nicest person to be around at times.

When we checked Evan into the hospital, we had just spent three hours driving from Austin to Dallas with a very manic little boy. I was scared, exhausted, and completely worn down. After an eternity (okay, 10 minutes, but it was a long 10 minutes) of waiting for someone in the children's psych unit to help us, a man in a polo shirt and khakis sauntered into the lobby, and very calmly said, "Well, hello there. And who are we here to see today?"

Are you kidding me? We were at the children's psych unit, not brunch. Evan was doing everything but smearing poop on the walls. It was pretty damned obvious who we were there to see. I lost it and completely raised my voice. The man chuckled and said, "I'm Dr. Diedrich, and I'll be the one treating your son."

Oops. I really didn't mean to lose it! I'm actually a very nice person. I was just at the end of my rope.

In that case, I didn't shock the doctor. He'd dealt with plenty of overwrought parents. When someone is suddenly rude as we're passing through the day, it's good to remember that person may be going through something terrible and normally doesn't act like that.

Conversely, there are some people who have no idea how to deal with adversity without making everyone around them miserable. They embrace the victim role and love the drama. When bad things happen to them, they wallow in it, tell everyone they know, and become super self-absorbed. They seem to attract misfortune and relish sharing their hardships with everyone they encounter.

Other people are just angry. Life seems unfair to them, and everyone else's portion looks better. They take out their anger on everyone around them.

Both of these kinds of people make life unpleasant for those around them, but truthfully, they make life the most miserable for themselves. They really don't know that there's another way to handle their circumstances.

Practice Kindness in the Face of Adversity

Many of us are stuck in our "stories." We tell ourselves a story over and over again about how life has been unfair and we have suffered unduly, and that other people—who don't suffer as we do—owe us for their pain. We're not trying to be obnoxious; we are acting according to what we really believe is right and proper for someone in our circumstances. We believe other people act differently because their circumstances are different.

In some ways, we're right. Some people really do find it easier to look on adversity as an opportunity. It isn't that these people have cushy lives. It's that when they're given pain, sickness, career setbacks, relationship problems, and other difficult circumstances, they look for the bright side, the opportunity to grow, or the chance to learn a new problem-solving skill. They take the difficult or pesky stuff in stride, and make the choice to focus on the positive rather than the negative.

Viewing challenges as opportunities is not an inherent trait for most of us. We learn it, either as children or as adults, by deliberately cultivating a different approach to adversity with new skills, behaviors, and ways of thinking. Anyone can learn to think and behave this way.

So if you're not a natural at finding opportunity in adversity, how do you do it?

First, observe how you see adversity. Do you see it as a personal attack against you or as a natural part of life?

A Taoist story tells of a farmer and his son who live in a village where horses are considered the greatest form of wealth. One day, a wild horse jumps into the farmer's field to graze on his crops. The son was very excited.

"Father!" he exclaimed, "this is wonderful!"

"Maybe," the father responded.

The next day the horse was gone. "Father!" cried the son, "this is horrible."

"Maybe" his father replied. But the very next day, the horse returned with many more from his herd. The son again was ecstatic with this good fortune. But his father responded with the same "maybe." The next day the boy went out and tried to ride one of the horses. It threw him and he broke his leg.

The son complained bitterly, saying, "The day those horses came was one of the worst days ever!" But his father responded exactly as he had before.

A week later, the military came through the village and conscripted all the young men, except for the boy with the broken leg.

You never know what seemingly bad circumstances may bring to your life. It's possible to accept adversity as a normal part of living.

Look for ways to handle adversity well. How can you be kind? How can you use this to strengthen your problem solving skills? What aspect of your character might be sharpened by learning to handle this situation differently?

Be kinder than necessary, for everyone you meet is fighting some kind of battle.—*T. H. Thompson and John Watson*

SLIGHT EDGE STRATEGY

- **Be compassionate:** Practice compassion toward people who are behaving poorly, knowing that they may be bearing burdens you can't see.

- **View challenges as opportunities:** Practice thinking about ways that you could use the difficult situations in your life to become stronger, wiser, kinder, more resourceful, and more resilient.

STRATEGY 20: Look for the Right Things

In our family, we play the slug bug game. When we're driving and we see a Volkswagen Beetle, we give each other a loving "nudge," and say "slug bug!"

When we started the game, I was amazed by how many slug bugs we found. Suddenly, the streets seemed full of Volkswagen Beetles. The number of Beetles hadn't actually changed. We found so many of them because we were searching for them. Many of us have had that experience: We're interested in a certain kind of car or house, we're thinking about a new logo for our company or a particular bike for our child's birthday—and all of a sudden they're everywhere!

This is the neurological phenomenon called selective attention or selective perception. When we're thinking hard about one thing, our brains tend to filter out all kinds of other stimuli so that we can see that one thing that we're looking for. The thing is that while selective attention works for slug bugs and fast food restaurant signs and other objects we're looking for, it also works for emotions and experiences and thoughts.

If you expect to see good, happy, friendly things, your selective attention will zero in on those things. It will filter out a lot of the negative stimuli that may be coming in around you, unnoticed. Conversely, if you're waiting for criticism, judgment, and unkindness, you may filter out a lot of wonderful things and only pick up on those negative ones.

One place I know this happens is during the beginning and ending stages of a relationship. When you meet someone you're infatuated with and you're in the honeymoon stage, you look for all of the wonderful things that person does, and you get flutters in your stomach every time they do one of those things. By the end of the relationship, you're looking for all of the things they do that make your skin crawl. Hell, watching them eat can be enough to make your stomach turn.

And that's just one relationship. Some people have their radars tuned to a specific frequency—positive or negative—in all of their interactions. At work, at home, in traffic, that one set of signals is the only set they pick up. What people say about their lives, associates, and families tells you a lot about what frequency they're tuned to.

I once heard a story about a man sitting on the porch of a general store. One day a family drove up and said "We're looking for a new town to move to. What is this town like?"

The man on the porch said, "Tell me about the town you came from."

"Oh," the husband replied. "It was horrible. The people were all rude and selfish and stupid. We had to get out of there."

"Well," the man on the porch answered, "this town's like that, too."

The husband's eyes opened wide. He said goodbye, and drove off. A few hours later, another family drove up.

"We're looking for a town in this area to move to because I got a new job here. What is this town like?"

The man on the porch leaned forward and said, "Tell me about the town you came from."

"Oh," the wife sighed, "We came from a great town. Everyone was so friendly and supportive, and we had so much fun at community gatherings. We'll miss it. We're hoping for a town similar to the wonderful town we left."

"Why, this town's just like that," said the man on the porch.

"Really? Great!" the family said, and went to tour the town.

The man on the porch knew that you get what you're looking for. If you're looking for kindness, generosity, and fun, you'll still have people around who are cranky and rude, but your brain will filter out a lot of what they throw at you. If you have your tuner set for negative, cranky behavior, then butterflies, rainbows, and unicorns could surround you and you will still see negativity.

I spent a long time wallowing in resentment toward God for giving me a child who had Evan's issues. I looked for reasons to be sad, reasons to be angry, and reasons to be resentful. Guess what? I found all of them in spades, and I was miserable.

When I started looking for the reasons I was blessed and could celebrate the life ahead of me, I found those, too.

My grandmother is one of the most amazing women I know. She is almost 90 years old, and every time I call her and ask how she's doing, she says, "Honey, if I were any better I'd be twins. At this point, Heaven is a lateral move!" I follow with, "Grammy, do you really feel that good?" She chuckles and says, "Hell no, honey! I hurt all over!" I always ask, "Grammy, how can you stay so positive?" She responds, "Well, honey, you find what you look for." Amen.

SLIGHT EDGE STRATEGY

- **Seek the positive:** Pay attention to what you tend to look for. Are you a glass half-full person or a glass half-empty person? Make a conscious choice to adjust your vision to see things in a positive light.

- **Create a visual reminder:** Write down inspirational notes to yourself to help you to remember to look for the right things, or look to your dream board for inspiration. (See Strategy 7 if you haven't yet created your dream board.) Keep these reminders in front of you. Remember, out of sight, out of mind.

STRATEGY 21: Dare to Dream

Think about it a minute.

If you had a guarantee and knew you couldn't fail—some kind of magic that would let you succeed—what would you do? Would you start a company? Write a book? Jump out of an airplane? Change careers? Move to Australia? Fall in love?

If you would do these things if you couldn't fail, what's stopping you from doing it now? Fear of failure. Have you ever stopped to think about what that failure might actually cost, and what it's costing to not even try? What would failure look like? Why would it be so bad to fail? Most people have failed lots of times, including creators of world-changing inventions. Failure in and of itself isn't a bad thing. It is simply figuring out what you don't want to repeat.

The problem with risking failure is fear. I don't even think of it as fear anymore. I think of it as FEAR: False Evidence Appearing Real.

Before I took Evan to the hospital, I had been working with the same consulting firm for more than 10 years. I had dreamed of starting my own company, but I was overcome by FEAR. What if I couldn't figure out how to build a website? How would I invoice clients? How would I market my business? The bigger question was what if I got out there and publicly tried to do something big and made mistakes that showed my weaknesses? What if I couldn't do it?

FEAR is usually based on a lack of information. It wasn't that I knew I *couldn't* build a website, it was that I knew absolutely nothing about building a website. Instead of actually sitting down with some books or scouring the Internet and researching what it took to build a business, all my thoughts about it were swallowed in anxious feelings. What if I tried and failed at some or all of it? My dream would be squished, and then what? As long as I didn't try, I hadn't failed. I could always think *maybe next year…*

A lot of us live our whole lives thinking *maybe next year…*

It took a traumatic, life changing experience for me to realize that I could actually do it. If I could manage having Evan in a pediatric psych unit and live at the Ronald McDonald House for two months, I was convinced I could handle anything.

Of course I still didn't know how to build a business. But I had spent so long avoiding taking Evan to the hospital because of a list of fears I had in my head—all of which had been unfounded—that I now knew I couldn't listen to those fears for my big decisions anymore.

So ask yourself, "What would I try if I knew I couldn't fail?" Or, what would you do if you knew you might fail at first, but eventually you'd achieve your dream? How many attempts would you be willing to make?

Every really important endeavor requires an element of risk. What would you be willing to risk to really go for your dreams? Here are some strategies for overcoming FEAR.

1. **Do your homework:** Spend some time researching the thing you want to try. What do you need to know in order to make a decision to go forward?

2. **Manage your risk:** What risks will you face? What can you do to mitigate those risks?

3. **Conquer in baby steps:** Break down your goal into small, manageable steps. Thinking about the final goal is key to achieving it, but you can't do it all at once. Take one step at a time.

4. **Give yourself permission to succeed:** Sometimes we have voices in our head that tell us there's no way we can have the thing we dream of. Be aware of those voices and be ready to dismiss them.

5. **Recruit a cheerleader:** Enlist supportive people—a spouse, a friend—to hold you accountable to your dream.

At the end of the day you have a choice. You can live in FEAR, or you can make the decision not to let it stand in the way of your dreams.

I recently heard a story about a woman sitting in a TV studio audience talking to the host, a motivational speaker. "I would really love to go to medical school, but I'm 50 years old," she said. "I'll be 54 when I get out!" The speaker replied, "You'll be 54 anyway."

SLIGHT EDGE STRATEGY

- **Face your fears:** What has been holding you back? What has been standing in your way? Why?

- **Dream big:** Write a list of things you would try if knew you wouldn't fail. The sky's the limit.

- **Take a risk:** Pick one item from your list above. What can you do to move closer to your goal? What steps can you take to accomplish this goal?

Part Two:

LIFE LOVE & WORK

STRATEGY 22: Set Clear Expectations

Unless I replace it, the toilet paper roll in our house runs the risk of being put on in the *wrong* direction when it's changed. I am an "over"—as in "spin the roll to find the end of the paper, and be on your way." I believe that, unless you have kids or cats, there's really no reason why the paper should hang under the roll. Every time I find it hung wrong, I sigh, roll my eyes, and change it back to the way it *should* be. Perhaps you can relate (unless you're a guy, in which case you're just happy there's toilet paper).

Why do I get so frustrated? Because my family doesn't meet my expectations. Have I ever told them that it bothers me? Nope. Have I ever explained how the toilet paper *should* go? Nope. I just assume they should know.

Last summer, I was outside grilling hamburgers for dinner. A few weeks before, Jay had cleaned the grill, and this was the first time we had used it since. As I started to flip the burgers, I looked down and saw my 20-pound white fluffy dog, Bernie, sitting under where the grease pan should have been, and catching every drop. I ran into the house and yelled to Jay, "Who cleans the grill and doesn't replace the grease pan?" Without missing a beat, he yelled back, "Who grills dinner without checking to see if there's a grease pan?"

I often catch myself making a whole lot of assumptions and holding people to expectations that I may not have clearly explained in the first place. I'll bet you do, too.

Whether it's toilet paper, an important project, or simply picking something up at the grocery store, most people don't fail to meet your expectations because they can't, don't care, or don't know how. Most people fail to meet your expectations because you never clearly communicated what they were in the first place.

We all get frustrated when our expectations aren't met. The question you have to stop and ask yourself is, "Did I clearly communicate what I expected?"

Once I was working with the CEO of a large company in Dallas and asked her what she did over a holiday weekend. She shared that she had four nephews—all under age 10—come for a visit.

When I asked how she could manage all of that, she said, "It was easy. I just let them know what my expectations were, and they got to choose whether or not they met them." Huh? How could it be that easy? Could this woman leap tall buildings in a single bound? Did she have a magical lasso that made people tell the truth? Was she a wizard?

She assured me that anyone could do this and proceeded to explain how the concept came to be. Several years of frustrating visits led her to an idea. She was tired of micromanaging the kids' behavior all weekend and wanted a more enjoyable and relaxed visit. She got a poster board, wrote their names across the top and stapled a $5 bill under each of their names. Then there was a list of rules:

- No jumping off the roof.
- No swearing.
- No yelling.
- No biting.
- No screaming.
- No peeing in the pool.

If *any* of the boys broke a rule, *all* of them lost a quarter. At the end of the visit, they got to keep however much money they had left. *That was it!*

She explained that at first, it was a challenge. After the first hour, they had to add a new rule: no tattling! By the end of the first day, the kids were actually policing each other and making sure they were all following the rules. She believed the kids didn't meet her expectations on previous visits, not because they didn't want to or couldn't, but because they didn't know what the expectations were.

If you subscribe to my philosophy that adults are just big versions of kids, it stands to reason that if this concept worked for kids, it is sure to work for adults. What if all of this time we have been getting frustrated with people for something we can prevent?

To ensure you are setting clear expectations (whether personally or professionally), try the following strategies:

1. **Know what you want before you get frustrated:** This is often the most difficult step. Many times, we haven't clarified in our own minds what we want, yet we assume others are being thoughtless or selfish when they don't satisfy our needs.

2. **Clearly communicate these expectations and, when necessary, ensure understanding:** Simply saying, "Do you understand?" is not ensuring understanding. Whether you ask the person to paraphrase, summarize, or re-explain, it is helpful to hear the other person reflect what they heard, to make sure you are on the same page.

3. **Define your desired outcome:** What do you want the end product or behavior to look like? How would you define success?

4. **Explain what you do want, rather than what you don't:** We have a tendency to complain about the actions and behaviors we don't like, when in reality, we haven't explained the actions and behaviors we would like to see.

5. **Reward the positive and coach the negative:** Whether at work or at home, remember that people repeat behavior that gets attention. If your expectations are met, make sure you say thank you or show appreciation. If your expectations are not met, before assuming the person intentionally disappointed you, make sure you communicated what you wanted clearly.

Remember, we usually find what we're looking for. If we look for the ways someone doesn't meet our expectations, we'll find them.

SLIGHT EDGE STRATEGY

- **Set and communicate expectations:** Every time you find yourself getting frustrated with someone this week, ask yourself if you set clear expectations and communicated them effectively. If not, take a deep breath, step back, and try again.

- **Identify an experience from your life:** When have you become frustrated because someone didn't meet your expectations? Did you communicate them clearly? Did you ensure understanding? What can you do next time to communicate your expectations up front?

STRATEGY 23: Draw Clear Boundaries

I'm not sure when we first started talking about boundaries as something we create to protect ourselves as a person. It might have been in the 1990s. At that time, a lot of people mocked the idea—especially those who had no boundaries and didn't want anyone else to have them either.

What's a boundary? It is a limit we set in relationships that allows us to protect ourselves. It lets those around us know what is acceptable and what is not. It means, "I will go this far, and no further."

Some people seem to have no boundaries at all, or very permeable ones. They don't put any protection around their own time, money, or emotions, so they are often depleted and hoping to pull some time, money, or emotional strength from us. The opposite extreme, of course, is someone whose boundaries preclude them ever helping anyone.

Most of us fall somewhere in the middle. It's often tough for us to decide whether our boundaries are balanced, too lenient, or too rigid. And it doesn't help that other people tend to chime in with their own ideas about the right boundary line: "You're not going to let your son

I recently told my mom I was going to take her to see a soccer game. When she asked why, I explained that I was going to show her what boundaries look like. When she said she didn't see any, I rubbed her arm and lovingly (and sarcastically) said, "I know."—Amy Schumer

move in **again**, are you?" or "You're really going to let your boss speak to you like that?"

A lot of us learned our boundaries growing up. If we had parents who expected us to enable them—like alcoholic parents or parents with emotional issues—we might believe it's our job or our identity to take care of other people before taking care of ourselves, or we might be so fed up with being the caregiver we don't want to help anybody, *ever*!

There isn't really one boundary that's right for every person and every situation. However, a pretty good standard rule is asking yourself this: Is this money, time, or emotional energy something that will cost me my ability to take care of myself?

Is helping this person with a project going to make you miss your deadlines? Is lending that person money going to make you have trouble covering your own financial responsibilities? Is helping that person cope with her failing marriage going to put a strain on your other relationships? Has this person come to you more than once asking for this kind of time, energy, or other costly investment into his or her well-being before?

If so, you may need to redefine your boundaries. We all have our own journey. We can't walk someone else's journey for them, and no one else can walk ours. We can help out here and there, but we all have our own set of troubles, drama, and tragedy. That's just part of life.

On an airplane if the oxygen mask drops down, you're instructed to put on your own mask first, then help your child or others put on theirs. That's because if you aren't breathing and conscious, you won't be able to help your child. If you aren't managing your own responsibilities first, both you and the person you're helping could be in trouble.

Not sure whether your boundaries are in the right place? Here are a few ways to help you figure it out:

1.   **Do a self-check:** Are you enabling a negative behavior, covering for someone else's repeated mistakes, or feel repeatedly taken advantage of? Most of the time, people won't treat us in a way we don't allow, at least not more than once. What could you be doing to enable that behavior?

2. **Identify your fear:** If you haven't set a clear limit or boundary, it's generally because you're afraid of something. Ask yourself, "What's the worst that could happen?" Be realistic. If you imagine the world ending because you said no, then you haven't really thought it through.

3. **Practice assertiveness:** Whether we are passive, passive-aggressive, or just plain aggressive, most of us have trouble being assertive. Some examples of assertive statements are: "I really need some space right now," "It's not okay for you to speak to me like that," "I'd rather you not email me outside of work," etc. If being assertive doesn't come naturally to you, you have to practice until it becomes a habit.

4. **Take care of you:** If you're one of those people who always puts others first, remember, you can't take care of someone else unless you take care of yourself first. Not only is it okay to protect and care for yourself, it's your responsibility.

SLIGHT EDGE STRATEGY

- **Determine your boundaries:** Take a look at what boundaries you have set up for yourself. Are you someone who wants to be there for others at any time, no matter the cost? Or do you have ways to protect your own resources while helping others when you can?

- **Strengthen your borders:** Identify one boundary that needs to be set a little tighter. Create a strategy and plan for how you will handle it the next time that boundary is crossed.

STRATEGY 24: Change Yourself First

In the space below, write the word "change."

_____

Now, write the word "change" with your other hand.

_____

What was the difference? Unless you are ambidextrous, it was probably more difficult and awkward with your non-dominant hand. It probably took longer, and it most likely did not look as neat. We are not used to writing with the other hand, and it requires change.

Change is often awkward, messy, difficult, and uncomfortable. Behavior changes one of three ways: rarely, slowly, or never.

Think of the last major attitude or behavior shift you've made. It probably took a great deal of effort to get out of your comfort zone and learn new habits. If it is so incredibly difficult to change our own behavior, why do we think we can change the behavior of others? The truth is, if there is an attitude or behavior you want to change in others, you must start by changing the way **you** think and behave. This is a tough one. You may ask, "Why do I have to be the one to change? They're the ones with the problem!" Because when it's all said and done, you can only control your actions and behavior.

Harvard Women's Health Watch published an article that said successful change is self-motivated and focused on positive outcomes rather than on negative ones, like guilt.[12] Hmm. That's pretty much the exact opposite of saying, "You need to change because there's something **wrong** with you."

---

[12]"Why It's Hard to Change Unhealthy Behavior—And Why You Should Keep Trying," _Harvard Women's Health Watch_ (January 2007), available at www.health.harvard.edu/newsweek/Why-its-hard-to-change-unhealthy-behavior.htm.

It reminds me of the Charlie Brown cartoon where Lucy said, "I would like to change the world!" Charlie Brown asked, "Where would you start?" Lucy replied, "I would start with you!"

The article also pointed out that change is a process, not an event, and it has several stages:

- **Pre-contemplation**, the first stage, occurs when you're not even consciously thinking about making a change, except to possibly defend your right not to make a change. You avoid thinking about the behavior because it makes you feel bad. To get to the place of actually doing something about it, you have to sense that it conflicts with other important goals you have.

- **Contemplation** is the next stage, when you acknowledge that the behavior is a problem and you may think of making a change, but you're not quite ready to act. This phase can go on for a long time.

- **Preparation** is the point at which you've acknowledged the behavior has to change, but you're gearing yourself up for it. This might mean coming to grips with the emotional fallout of giving up drinking or smoking, looking for a gym to join, learning about time management, and putting the tools in place. It can involve many layers of your life and requires strategies to overcome obstacles before you can launch into your action plan.

- **Action** is, well, action. You start walking 20 minutes a day, spend more evenings with your family, tuck money into your savings account, whatever it is that requires your action. This is the vulnerable time when you see the challenges of life without that old behavior. At this point, the more support you have the better.

- **Maintenance** is when, after you've been practicing the new behavior for a while, you just have to keep it going. Everyone relapses periodically, but you jump back on the horse and press on. You may find you need to develop other new behaviors to support this one.

Now, given that change involves all of these emotionally, mentally, physically, and sometimes logistically challenging maneuvers, how often are any of us really likely to get someone else to walk through that process?

The only way Evan changed was for me to change first…a lot. First I had to change my attitude about taking him to the hospital. Then I had to become a lot more consistent and self-disciplined about keeping him on eating and medication schedules, responding to inappropriate behavior, and watching what came out of my mouth when I was frustrated. Because I changed, Evan responded differently.

It may be that you have a coworker or partner, and the two of you just keep pushing each other's hot buttons (more on those in Strategy 36) without even realizing you're doing it. You both have needs that aren't being met or frustrations that are being exacerbated. It's like some Three Stooges skit where you both just keep poking one another expecting that this poke will be the one that makes the difference. It almost becomes a game, although not a very enjoyable one.

Unless you want to play the game forever, you have to step back and see what you can change. Maybe at first you just hold your tongue instead of jabbing back. See what response that evokes. You would be surprised at what a big difference those little changes on your side can create. If you can get a little distance, sometimes you gain perspective on what has caused your dynamic and how to change it so you don't have to play that stressful game anymore. Then you can communicate more honestly.

Here's a warning though: Sometimes people get upset when you change, even if they've been saying they want you to make that change. One of the principles of programs like Al-Anon is that someone involved with an alcoholic must change him or herself first, and sometimes the act of one person getting healthier makes the whole construct of the relationship fall apart. Change is hard, even when it's good. Evan wasn't exactly thrilled with the new, consistent Mommy because it required him to change, too. On the other hand, it's nice to know that your best path to peace is in your own hands—changing you, your thoughts, and your actions.

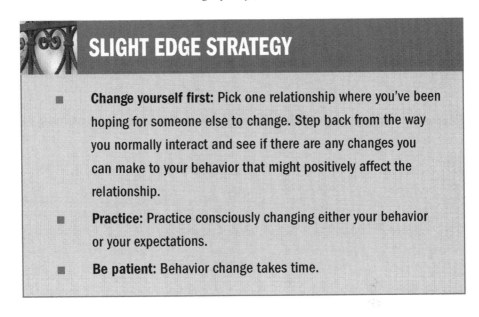

SLIGHT EDGE STRATEGY

- **Change yourself first:** Pick one relationship where you've been hoping for someone else to change. Step back from the way you normally interact and see if there are any changes you can make to your behavior that might positively affect the relationship.

- **Practice:** Practice consciously changing either your behavior or your expectations.

- **Be patient:** Behavior change takes time.

STRATEGY 25:
Maintain a Positive Balance

Everything in our lives boils down to energy. We are either giving energy, or we are taking energy away. This is true of every task, responsibility, and interaction. I never realized how physically, emotionally, and mentally exhausted I was until Evan was hospitalized. The nights we spent at the Ronald McDonald House while he was in the inpatient unit were the first times we were able to be without Evan and know he was safe. We didn't have to worry about phone calls notifying us of people he'd hurt, because we knew he was with trained staff that understood what we had been going through.

I remember going home to Austin visiting one of my friends for a night while Jay stayed in Dallas. She said I looked more rested and at peace than she'd ever seen me. That really hit home. Even though we were going through this traumatic experience, I hadn't felt this rested and at peace since before Evan was born. I never realized it, but so many of our interactions had taken a major withdrawal from my emotional bank account. Much of our time together was sapping my energy. I had been running on empty for a long time, and my engine was shot.

In his book *7 Habits of Highly Effective People*,[13] Stephen Covey introduced the concept of the emotional bank account. Similar to a regular bank account, we make deposits and withdrawals in our relationships, only these are on an emotional level, and the stakes are much higher.

In our relationships, we typically start off with a neutral balance, and it is our choice to make emotional deposits or withdrawals. The challenge many of us run into is that, much like our current economy,

---

[13]Stephen R. Covey, *The 7 Habits of Highly Effective People: Powerful Lessons in Personal Change* (New York: Simon and Schuster, 1989).

we borrow more than we have available and get so behind that it is difficult to catch up.

Think of the people in your life who are important to you. What's your balance? Have you continued to make deposits, building and strengthening relationships? When the other person in the relationship is making deposits at the same rate, the relationship flourishes. If, however, you perceive your deposits outweigh theirs or their withdrawals outweigh your deposits, you'll end up frustrated and the relationship suffers. Here are a few ways to ensure your balance remains positive:

1. **Be aware:** One of the best strategies to maintaining a positive balance is to be aware that the bank account exists. Sometimes, just an awareness that we must deliberately and consciously focus on this can make a big difference. If you're not sure where you stand with someone, ask. When we're worried about having money in our bank account, not checking the balance doesn't fix the situation. It's better to know where you stand.

2. **Do what you say you will do:** Whether it's a small promise or a big commitment, be counted on to be true to your word. Nothing withdraws faster from an emotional bank account than a lack of trust, accountability, and integrity.

3. **Operate with a 100 percent mindset:** Rather than making sure there is a 50/50 balance, take full responsibility for the success of the relationship. If we're not willing to take full ownership, we end up keeping score—no one wins when we do that.

4. **Make sure your deposit has value to the other person:** We might think we're the best thing around and that our deposits are overwhelmingly positive, but if our actions aren't meaningful to the other person, we're likely not going to get the results we want.

5. **The little deposits add up:** So do the little withdrawals. It's generally not one big deposit or withdrawal that determines the ending

balance of the account, rather the little ones made over a long time. Stay vigilant about monitoring your balance.

6. **Be there:** Sometimes, the biggest deposit you can make is just to be there if you're needed. While we were going through the hospitalization ordeal with Evan, the biggest deposits were made by those who simply said, "I'm here if you need me." Sometimes, that's all it takes.

7. **When you make a withdrawal, apologize and make it right:** We're all human, and we are all going to make withdrawals at one time or another. The late Randy Pausch—the Carnegie Mellon professor who chronicled his battle with terminal pancreatic cancer with wit and inspiration—said that most people do a lousy job of apologizing. He outlined an effective apology in three parts: (1) I'm sorry; (2) It was my fault; (3) How do I make it right?[14] Most of us screw up the last part, and that's the most important step.

Remain deliberate and conscious about the deposits and withdrawals you make into the accounts of the people in your life. Overdraft fees are much higher in these accounts.

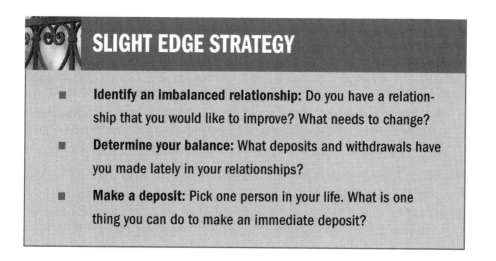

SLIGHT EDGE STRATEGY

- **Identify an imbalanced relationship:** Do you have a relationship that you would like to improve? What needs to change?

- **Determine your balance:** What deposits and withdrawals have you made lately in your relationships?

- **Make a deposit:** Pick one person in your life. What is one thing you can do to make an immediate deposit?

---

[14]Randy Pausch, *The Last Lecture* (New York: Hyperion, 2008).

STRATEGY 26: Share Your Perspective

I
n the movie *Hitchhiker's Guide to the Galaxy*, the protagonists search for an extraordinary weapon: a Point of View gun. If you shoot someone with this gun, he or she will instantly see things from your point of view. I want that gun.

But I don't have one, and I'm guessing you don't either. So our points of view, and the points of view of those around us always have to filter through our own biases and perspectives. This can make communicating, working with, and loving other people really challenging at times.

There was an interesting experiment about effectively communicating your point of view in the book *Made to Stick*.[15] The authors explored ways to make ideas and communication "stick." They explained a study in which a PhD candidate created a simple game where she assigned people one of two roles: tappers and listeners.

The tappers got a list of common songs that most of us know: "Happy Birthday," "The Star-Spangled Banner," "Old McDonald," etc. The listeners had to guess what song was being tapped. Simple, right?

The tappers anticipated that the listeners would guess the songs correctly 50 percent of the time when, in reality, they only got it right 2 percent of the time. The tappers grew increasingly frustrated with the listeners. How could they not guess "Happy Birthday" when tapped out on a table?

The researcher found it was due to "the curse of knowledge." Once we know something, it's hard to imagine what it was like to not know it. Because the tappers knew what song they were tapping, they actually

---

[15]Chip Heath and Dan Heath, *Made to Stick* (New York: Random House, 2007).

heard the song in their heads. It was impossible for them not to hear the song when tapping, which made it difficult to understand why the listener couldn't figure out the song.

Name That Tune

We have worlds of knowledge, as well as opinions, experiences, and perceptions in our heads that we assume are shared, just like the tappers assumed that people could hear "Old MacDonald" out of a series of taps. We can't share all of that information every time we want to communicate an idea—meetings would never end. It is possible, though, when we're talking about something and the other person doesn't understand, that there's some perspective, back story, or experience that we have playing in our heads that we're not communicating.

Some of these experiences are going to be easier to share than others. When you're discussing one approach to a project versus another, you might have history that says you've tried one way to do the project and it failed. You want to steer around that. That is a tune you can easily share with the other person so they can hear what you're thinking. The other person still might want to come up with alternatives, but you've got one piece of information to communicate. Once you communicate that, the other person can hear the song in your head.

Other situations require more complex communication. Perhaps you've been in a bad relationship before, and you are nervous about getting hurt. Maybe you were passed up for a promotion and are still feeling bitter. Regardless of the situation, it is your responsibility to help the other person hear the tune.

Suppose you have a team working on a project: one person is from IT, one is the CFO, and one is from marketing. Each knows the best practices in his or her area and each wants to succeed, yet each has a completely different perspective on how to tackle and accomplish the goal. Nobody's trying to thwart the team or cause the project to fail; it's just that each person has a very different tune in his or her head. It will take communication, not turf wars, to help make each person's point understood.

Other approaches are even more difficult to agree upon. The way families interact, for example, tends to be so ingrained that you may think the way you do it is normal and your partner's approach is weird or wrong. You may assume that family can visit whenever they like because, hey, they're family! Your spouse, however, may think family should call ahead, make sure it's convenient, and accept "No, it's not a good time right now" without getting offended.

One big step in the right direction is to try to make sure the other person or other people understand your fundamental goals. You also need to impart any information or history you have that is specifically shaping your perspective on the issue.

Take time to listen and understand the goals of others, and identify information or history that is helping to frame their point of view. Ask clarifying questions and try to understand where they are coming from. Then explain your viewpoint, share your perspective, and help others understand your frame of reference. When you've both shared the music in your heads, you're a lot more likely to be able to harmonize.

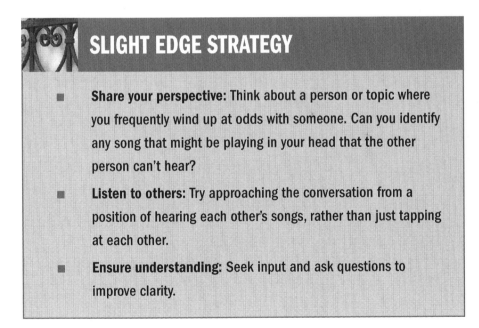

SLIGHT EDGE STRATEGY

- **Share your perspective:** Think about a person or topic where you frequently wind up at odds with someone. Can you identify any song that might be playing in your head that the other person can't hear?

- **Listen to others:** Try approaching the conversation from a position of hearing each other's songs, rather than just tapping at each other.

- **Ensure understanding:** Seek input and ask questions to improve clarity.

STRATEGY 27: Get It Right

Eighty-five percent of our success is attributed to our ability to effectively communicate and maintain healthy relationships. Only 15 percent of financial and career success stems from our technical abilities. Interpersonal communication skills determine our success both personally and professionally.[16]

Although many of us have had some kind of communication training and we've got the mechanics down, when it comes to difficult conversations, the most important factor is one that's seldom taught: negotiating for the best outcome. That is, what is our goal in this conversation? Are we out to share perspectives and reach the best decision? Or do we just want to win? Is our goal to be right or get it right?

Of course most of us would say we want to get it right, but deep down, what we mean is, "as long as I get to *be* right in the process."

One of Evan's therapists told me something that changed my life. She said, "You can't have a power struggle alone." It's amazing how one sentence transformed the way I managed Evan, and several other relationships. It is so true. It is impossible to play tug of war alone.

Now when Evan starts a power struggle with me over something he wants, I step back and analyze: What is it he's really asking for? Often it's not what he's demanding. It might seem like he is deliberately trying to annoy me by poking his fingers in my face, but he's really craving attention. What can I give him that doesn't drain my time or emotional bank account and that's actually in his best interest? How can we both win? Therein lies the solution. I don't get into the battle any more. I don't have to win and he doesn't have to lose in the process. Whether you're

---

[16]Keld Jensen, "Intelligence Is Overrated: What You Really Need to Succeed," *Forbes* (April 12, 2012), available at www.forbes.com.

dealing with a six-year-old or a 60-year-old, the same concepts apply. In a challenging communication situation, step back and think about your goal for the communication.

■ Do you want a decision to go a specific way? What obstacles might prevent that from happening?

■ What are the other person's goals, and how can you help the other person get what he or she wants while not completely forfeiting what you need?

■ What is a mutual goal you are both striving toward? For example, if the question is who is going to take the lead on a project, are you both looking for status and recognition? How can you both accomplish that? If the question is where your family is going on vacation, identify some important factors that you and your partner need, and reach a compromise where both of your needs are met.

■ How can you both walk away with a win?

■ How is your approach affecting the way the discussion goes?

We are all born with innate communication styles, and our environment shapes how those styles develop. Some people learn to play the passive role, trying to stay out of conflict and wind up feeling disenfranchised. Others schmooze and manipulate, some demand and intimidate. Besides healthy ways of interacting there's a whole host of unhealthy ways. And then there's the gender gap.

Psychologist and researcher Deborah Tannen has done extensive studies on the differences between male and female communication. In her book *You Just Don't Understand*,[17] she explains some of the differences in the way men and women communicate:

■ Women communicate to foster intimacy; men communicate to foster independence.

■ Women seek understanding; men assume you're asking for advice.

---

[17]Deborah Tannen, *You Just Don't Understand: Women and Men in Conversation* (New York: HarperCollins, 1990).

- Women communicate feelings; men communicate information.

- Women seek proposals for discussion; men communicate orders or action items to get to the decision stage.

Of course this is not true for every man and every woman in every situation, but these are the general tendencies. A woman may make a suggestion by way of a question: "Do you want to be the lead on this project?" To which the man may answer "Yeah, great." She may be trying to open a discussion about who would be the best project lead and expect the man to ask her if she wants the position. Most men don't communicate that way, so he assumes she's offering him the lead and he takes it. Now she may be frustrated and either try to reopen the conversation or just fume at the arrogance of her coworker. He wasn't being arrogant. He thinks it's a straightforward question, so he answers it.

The more you can learn about communication styles, the easier it will be to frame a conversation in a way that leads to win-win outcomes—whether that's at work or at home. The most powerful thing to bring to a conversation is putting your desire to *get it right* ahead of your desire to *be right.*

Sarcastic word of caution: Do not tell your significant other that you are using this strategy. Jay will stop me in the middle of my occasional rant and say, "Honey, what's your goal? Are you trying to be right or get it right?" I'm always tempted to nonverbally communicate my dissatisfaction with a one-finger wave, but I usually bite my tongue, or my finger.

When it comes to survival strategies, communication tops my list. Whether it's communicating effectively with Evan, managing relationships with clients and family, or updating doctors and specialists, without effective communication, I would be dead in the water.

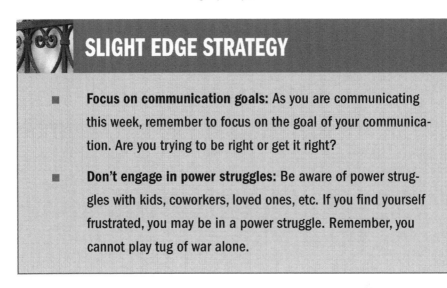

SLIGHT EDGE STRATEGY

■ **Focus on communication goals:** As you are communicating this week, remember to focus on the goal of your communication. Are you trying to be right or get it right?

■ **Don't engage in power struggles:** Be aware of power struggles with kids, coworkers, loved ones, etc. If you find yourself frustrated, you may be in a power struggle. Remember, you cannot play tug of war alone.

STRATEGY 28: Check Your Blind Spots

I was talking to someone after a presentation and she said, "All this leadership and communication stuff is great, but it doesn't really apply to me. Everyone likes me."

That may be true sister, but let's face it—you don't know what you don't know. We all have blind spots. A blind spot is a part of our personality or behavior that we're not aware of, yet others can see it. And regardless of our intelligence, emotional or otherwise, we all have them.

We can only see our behavior from our own point of view. Someone who sees her conversational style as self-confident and open may appear to others as condescending. Someone who perceives himself as an independent thinker and maverick may strike others as a poor collaborator. Someone who sees herself as the office confidant may be perceived by others as the office gossip.

Unfortunately, those blind spots might be the reason we don't get promoted when we think we've earned it. Our blind spots may explain why we lose customers or why our relationships don't work out. Until we know what those blind spots are, they may affect our lives without us even knowing it. That can lead to a lot of frustration and disappointment.

When you're driving, would you ever change lanes without checking your blind spot? Of course not. It could have dangerous, painful, and even permanent consequences. So why would you want to go through life missing opportunities because of a behavior you could have changed?

Sometimes we're not ready to face our blind spots. It's that facing fear of change thing again. If you're not ready to uncover them, that's okay. Ignorance is bliss, and sometimes we're not in a place to "work" on our own issues. Give yourself permission to not worry about it until it's something you can really focus on. When you're ready to change lanes, here are some suggestions for successfully checking your blind spots.

1. **Be choosy with whom you seek input:** This process can be emotionally difficult. It's jarring to learn what people have been thinking about you without your knowing it. Don't invite just anyone to give input. You may not want to hear from your super-critical friend who never fails to find what's wrong with other people. Ask people who know you and care about you and whose judgment you trust.

2. **Ask for positive feedback:** Ask for feedback about your strengths and good qualities. We are so quick to be self-critical. It's helpful to get an objective view of your perceived strengths and positive personality traits.

3. **Listen without getting defensive:** Giving feedback is risky for the people who provide it, so be grateful to those whose opinion you seek and try not to get defensive. Remember that you might hear things you don't agree with or that hurt your feelings. You asked for this, so really consider what they're saying. You can ask questions, but don't argue. If they're telling you that you have a particular trait, that's what they see. Telling them they're wrong won't change their perceptions; it will just protect your blind spot and ensure that they don't open up to you with this kind of feedback in the future.

4. **Pick one area and focus on it:** Don't bite off more than you can chew. It will become overwhelming and nothing will change. Instead, pick one thing that you can change. If someone tells you that you need too much help making decisions and that's keeping you from moving up in the management chain, start making small decisions on your own and work your way up. Read books and articles about decision making and good decision makers. Whatever it is, only tackle one area at a time.

5. **Seek ongoing feedback, and make it safe for people who provide it:** If you trusted the people who gave you feedback in the first place, you may be able to ask them to tell you, from time to time, if they see changes. Because this is your blind spot, it will be useful to seek an objective opinion on whether or not you're making progress. Again, resist the urge to argue or get defensive.

6. **It's a journey, not a destination:** No matter how enlightened we are, we will always have some blind spots, and that's okay. Continuously striving for progress is the goal.

Keep in mind that the people you love have blind spots, too. You may overlook them because, on the whole, you value them and they have many more positive traits than negative ones. When people tell you about your blind spots, it's unlikely that they've been stewing about them night and day without telling you. They've probably overlooked yours because of all of your wonderful qualities. This is not about unearthing every negative thing everyone thinks about you, it's about you taking a risk to grow and make your life as successful as it can be.

SLIGHT EDGE STRATEGY

- **Solicit feedback:** What feedback have you received in the past that might provide insight into your blind spots?

- **Pick a friend to help:** Identify a supportive and trusted friend that you believe will provide honest and candid feedback.

- **Bite the bullet:** When you're ready, sit down with this person, ask for feedback, listen, and take time to process.

- **Create a strategy:** Identify one step you can take to make small improvements.

STRATEGY 29: Identify Your Style

I f you've ever taken a behavioral assessment, like the Myers Briggs, Disc, Insights, Colors, Animals, etc., then you're probably familiar with the concepts I'm about to explain. If you haven't taken a behavioral assessment, now is your chance. Unfortunately you need a PhD to understand much of what's been written on the topic. I'm going to simplify it.

Although names and labels differ, ultimately, there are four primary behavior styles: Driver, Expressive, Amiable, and Analytical.

Everyone is a combination of styles, meaning no one is all one style or none of another. We all float along on a continuum. If you balance evenly across multiple styles, you are able to flex and adapt fairly easily to others. The downside is that you are not as likely to be consistent. Others may never know which version of you they are going to get, based on the day, the issue, the project, or mood. If you are more heavily weighted and dominant in one or two styles, the advantage is that you are consistent. People know what to expect from you. The downside? You have to work really hard to modify your style.

All of us can modify for short amounts of time. After that, we retreat into our comfort zones to recharge. Although no style is good or bad, when we are under stress, our styles become magnified so heavily that our strengths actually get overextended and become weaknesses.

For example, I love speaking to audiences, and when I'm in the zone, time flies. I could speak for an entire day and leave with more energy than I started with. However, when I'm with Evan, I have to use skills and behaviors that are not second nature to me. I have to monitor his behavior, medication, what I say, how I say it, and more. By nature, I am not generally a patient, detailed person, and I have to be exactly that with Evan. While I can speak for hours and feel energized, I often fall asleep right after putting Evan to bed after spending only three or four hours with him.

Although I have spent a lot of time feeling guilty for being exhausted around Evan, I have come to learn that it has nothing to do with my parenting ability or my love for him. It simply requires me to work outside of my comfort zone.

If, after certain tasks or activities, you feel like a vacuum has just sucked the life force from your body, you are working out of your comfort zone. It's not necessarily a bad thing, but it does require more focused attention and concerted energy.

It's important to understand that your style neither has to do with how educated you are (you could have a GED or a PhD and have the same style), nor how old you are (you could be eight or 80 and have the same style). Style isn't determined by moral turpitude, intelligence, or intent. Your style is merely a reflection of how you react, respond, and communicate. We are all born with predispositions to certain styles. Our environment then shapes and molds us.

I'm often asked if it's possible to be one style at work and another style at home. It really depends. If you are highly dominant in one or two styles, chances are you operate that way consistently wherever you go and whomever you're with. If you are fairly even in two or more styles, different people and situations are likely to bring out different elements of each style.

I'm going to briefly describe each style. Then I'll show you how to determine someone's style simply by observing them. Finally, I'll provide some techniques on how to effectively communicate with each of the styles. I'll refer back to these periodically with suggestions on productivity, conflict resolution, goal setting, and more.

Take the informal behavior style assessment on the next page to get a general idea of your style.

Behavior Style Assessment

Identify your basic communication style by completing the informal assessment on the next page. In each box, circle the words that best describe your personality. Circle any word that feels "right." In other words, don't overthink it! To obtain a more complete assessment of your basic communication style, ask one or more other people who know you well to complete an inventory about you. Be sure to ask someone you can trust to be objective.

BEHAVIOR STYLE ASSESSMENT

DRIVER	▪ Action Oriented ▪ Bold ▪ Competitive ▪ Controlling ▪ Decisive	▪ Industrious ▪ Self-reliant ▪ Serious ▪ Strong Willed Total _____
EXPRESSIVE	▪ Ambitious ▪ Energetic ▪ Excitable ▪ Friendly ▪ Fun Loving	▪ Intuitive ▪ Optimistic ▪ Motivator ▪ Spontaneous Total _____
AMIABLE	▪ Adaptable ▪ Calm ▪ Cooperative ▪ Good Listener ▪ Enjoys Routine	▪ Loyal ▪ Patient ▪ Sensitive Feelings ▪ Tolerant Total _____
ANALYTICAL	▪ Accurate ▪ Cautious ▪ Conscientious ▪ Detailed ▪ Enjoys Instructions	▪ Factual ▪ Impersonal ▪ Inquisitive ▪ Logical Total _____

To score, count the number of words you circled and write that number on the line. Then transfer the corresponding behavior styles to the spaces below.

Top Two Communication Styles: _____ / _____

To download a complete version of the style assessment, visit my website at www.annegradygroup.com/assessment.

It's important to remember that no style is right or wrong, good or bad, or better or worse than any other style. We all have elements of each style to varying degrees in different situations. This assessment is an extremely informal tool with a possible score of 9 in each of the styles. Even though more sophisticated assessments are available, this one will give you a general idea of your dominant and back-up styles.

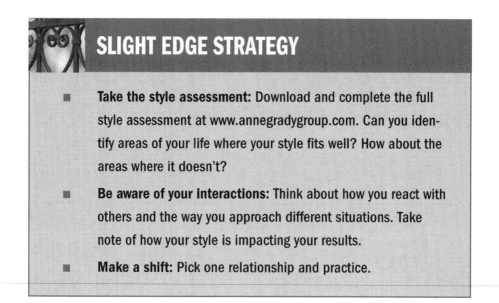

SLIGHT EDGE STRATEGY

- **Take the style assessment:** Download and complete the full style assessment at www.annegradygroup.com. Can you identify areas of your life where your style fits well? How about the areas where it doesn't?

- **Be aware of your interactions:** Think about how you react with others and the way you approach different situations. Take note of how your style is impacting your results.

- **Make a shift:** Pick one relationship and practice.

STRATEGY 30:
Get to Know the Four Styles

Now that you've identified your dominant style(s), it's time to look a little closer. The characteristics I detail here are the basics of the four styles. These are only tendencies and are not meant to define you or pigeonhole you. Use them more as a frame of reference.

Drivers

Drivers walk fast, talk fast, eat fast, think fast, multitask, and focus on getting results. Drivers like to be in control and appreciate when others share their sense of urgency. The Drivers' motto? If it ain't broke, break it, because I can make it work quicker, faster, easier, and better.

Drivers are big-picture thinkers and are extremely decisive. They sometimes make careless errors or make decisions without having all the information. They typically have a short fuse and get angry easily, but they get over it just as fast. In other words, a Driver might tell you you're stupid and your mother's ugly, leave you bleeding on the sidewalk with your jugular exposed, and then ask you out for drinks all within the same hour.

Drivers tend to be extroverted. They think and process aloud, so they often say things they regret. Because Drivers are results-oriented, task driven, and assertive, when they are under stress and pressure, they can come across as rude, aggressive, or abrasive.

Drivers are not typically detail-oriented. They don't care how the clock was made, they just want to know the time, and they want to know now.

Drivers like to be in control. They know what they want, and they accomplish a lot in a short amount of time. They often think strategically, rather than tactically.

Their words can sting, they make careless errors, and decisions aren't always well thought-out. However, drivers are go-getters, love to be competitive, and are extremely productive.

Expressives

Like Drivers, Expressives are big-picture thinkers, fast-paced, and impatient. They are also extroverted, process aloud, and prefer the big picture to details. Unlike Drivers, Expressives are more focused on people and relationships than results. They enjoy social situations and interacting with others.

Expressives are sharers. They will come into work on Monday and walk around the office telling everyone what happened from the time they left the office on Friday until they drove in the parking lot that morning. (And they have pictures to prove it!)

Expressives are storytellers, they are persuasive, and they enjoy being the center of attention. Because they move fast and focus on the big picture, they tend to make careless errors and miss details.

Validation, feedback, and recognition are crucial to Expressives. They struggle with social rejection and hate when others appear upset with them.

Expressives appear disorganized, tend to have lots of piles, start on the next task before finishing the one they are working on, and get bored easily. They are emotional, highly social, extremely persuasive, and enjoy building relationships and fun environments. They are the reason you have happy hour!

Amiables

In contrast to Drivers and Expressives, Amiables and Analyticals are slow-paced, patient, introverted, and detail-oriented.

Amiables are all about harmony and peace. They are extremely loyal, and they are great listeners. Amiables are team-players who love doing things to help others. Amiables don't like to be the center of attention, but they do want to know they are making a difference.

Amiables prefer consistency. Drivers would drive 20 miles out of their way just to avoid sitting in traffic, whereas Amiables are more patient and prefer predictable routines.

Amiables are also indecisive. Have you ever seen two Amiables trying to go to lunch? "Where do you want to go?" "Wherever you want to go," says the other Amiable." Well what do you like to eat?" "Whatever you like to eat," says the other Amiable. The Driver has already eaten and the Expressive is still sharing stories about their favorite restaurant.

Amiables dislike conflict, confrontation, and change. In an effort to avoid conflict, Amiables tend to be passive-aggressive. Rather than assertively communicate how they're feeling, they'll take it, and take it, and take it—until, like a rubber band, they've stretched too far, and then they pop. Because it has taken them so long to get to the point of being upset, it takes them a long time to get over their anger, and they often hold a grudge.

Have you ever asked Amiables how they're doing when they are clearly upset, and they respond with, "I'm fine!" (and you know they're not)? I've sometimes foolishly said, "Really? You should tell your face." The results were never quite what I was going for.

Analyticals

Similar to Amiables, Analyticals are very patient, slow-paced, and detail-oriented. Analyticals also tend to be more introverted, meaning they gain their energy by spending time alone, having time to think and process. Analyticals are similar to Drivers in that their main focus is on results, but they prefer to focus on quality, detail, and accuracy, regardless of how long the task takes.

Analyticals prefer to collect all of the information, examine all sides of the equation, and carefully and methodically make a decision. This can be frustrating for Drivers and Expressives who would rather make a quick decision, even if it requires going back and making adjustments later.

Analyticals may appear to be skeptical and critical, as they ask a lot of questions and challenge information. They are simply trying to gather data and understand. Because they spend a great deal of time and energy ensuring their results are accurate, they tend to become defensive when others point out mistakes or oversights.

Similar to Drivers, Analyticals are extremely logical and objective. They are not as likely to be persuaded by feelings and emotions but prefer logic and facts. Analyticals tend to be black-and-white thinkers, uncomfortable with shades of gray.

Let's say an Expressive asks an Analytical a question about a policy or a procedure. The Analytical is likely to answer in a flat tone, "Really? It's on page 456, second paragraph, before the hyphen, after the semicolon. It clearly states our policy. Why don't you just look it up?" The Expressive then answers, "Why would I look it up when I can just ask you?"

SLIGHT EDGE STRATEGY

- **Observe those around you:** Do you see any of the behavior style characteristics in the people you live with, work with, and interact with most often?

- **Consider your personal style:** Continue to pay attention to your responses, reactions, and tendencies. How do you like to communicate? What are your reactions to stress? What styles do you feel attracted to/repelled by?

- **Keep a journal:** Pick a couple of relationships and take note of how others' behaviors make you feel. Do you see any patterns?

STRATEGY 31:
Explore Style Combinations

Most of us are not just one style. We are combinations of styles that bring out some interesting results. Remember, no style is good or bad, right or wrong. No style is better at parenting, relationships, work, life, or love. They each have strengths and weaknesses. Understanding style combinations gives us the ability to understand the subtleties that make us react, respond, and communicate the way we do.

Armed with this knowledge, we can influence others to create positive outcomes for everyone involved.

Driver/Analytical

If you're a Driver/Analytical—meaning those two styles are your highest scores—you can balance speed and efficiency with precision and accuracy. Because both styles tend to like to be in control and are goal-oriented, yours is a very strong personality. The benefit is that you get a whole lot done, and it's quality work. The downside is that you might rub people the wrong way, appearing cold or uncaring when focusing on achieving results. In a work setting, Driver/Analyticals may get frustrated by the other styles' need to socialize. After all, you are here to do a job and can make friends outside of work if you choose. It certainly doesn't mean you don't value relationships. You are just primarily motivated by results and outcomes.

To maximize your style: Continue to focus on results, but temper that with other people's need for relationship building. Make time for a little small talk and engage with others about non-work related issues.

Driver/Expressive

If you're a Driver/Expressive, you are most likely a fast-paced, big-picture thinker. You tend to be impulsive, jumping from task to task, get frustrated when others don't keep up, and shy away from details. You get a lot done and have fun doing it. Unfortunately, you may miss a lot of details and make careless errors in the process. The Driver/Expressive is extroverted, social, and outgoing. You are a very strong personality and are able to balance relationships with results. A woman at one of my presentations came up to me after my session and said, "The Driver/Expressive is kind of like a seagull. They fly in, stir stuff up, crap on everything, and then leave." My reaction? "How do you know me so well?!"

To maximize your style: Realize that not everyone moves at your pace, and that's okay. Practice patience, make an effort to finish one task before starting another, and spend a little more time focused on the details. Resist the urge to take control and dominate conversations.

Driver/Amiable

If you're a Driver/Amiable, you struggle internally. You need to be in control and get results, but you don't want to hurt others' feelings or appear rude or overbearing. You are able to find balance between results and relationships but often have to fight your own nature to listen without taking over. As a result, balancing both tendencies, you wind up operating at a moderate pace.

To maximize your style: Resist the temptation to have to accomplish things your way (refer to Strategy 27). Even if you don't agree with the other person's approach, will it help accomplish the goal? If so, go with it. Focus on being assertive, rather than passive-aggressive.

Expressive/Amiable

If you are an Expressive/Amiable, you are all about relationships. You're moderately paced, balancing the need for results with time to process and gather information. The Expressive/Amiable is a great listener, always looking for ways to be supportive and nurturing. You may frustrate Drivers and Analyticals because they tend to be less emotional and more objective, but in your mind, building relationships takes precedence over results.

To maximize your style: While relationships are most definitely important, make sure that you aren't sacrificing results because of them. Stay focused on what needs to be accomplished and communicate assertively to those around you. Shy away from combat, but embrace healthy conflict.

Expressive/Analytical

If Expressive and Analytical are your two highest scores, you feel a similar struggle as the Driver/Amiable. You have the best of both styles, wanting to be fun, share stories, and be the center of attention, while also feeling the need to be extremely detail-oriented. You have a tendency to want things done your way and often become emotional when not getting the desired result.

To maximize your style: Realize that when you question people about what they are doing or the way they are doing it, it could be perceived as critical or judgmental. Resist the temptation to have the last word or the expectation that things have to be done your way.

Amiable/Analytical

If you're an Amiable/Analytical, you're the most deliberate, slow-paced, and patient of all of the combinations. Craving a great deal of information and detail, and needing a lot of time to process it, the Amiable/Analytical can frustrate others who want faster results. You tend to be more introverted, quiet, and contemplative. You take time to process and understand the world around you.

To maximize your style: Make sure you occasionally come out of your comfort zone, being more expressive and assertive about what you need and want. While it may be difficult initially, you'll become more assertive with practice, and it will lead to better results.

One Piece of the Equation

All of the explanations above are simply tendencies, meaning you could have two people with exactly the same style combination, and they may have very different personality traits. Many variables go into making us who we are, and behavior style is merely one component of that equation. Your style, however, does provide insight into the way you perceive the world, manage your time, deal with conflict, and so much more.

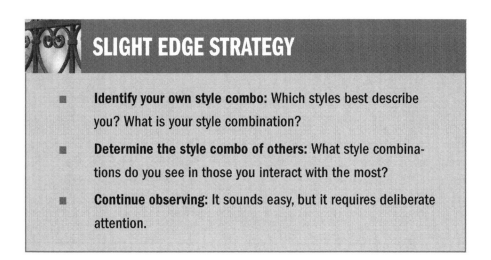

SLIGHT EDGE STRATEGY

- **Identify your own style combo:** Which styles best describe you? What is your style combination?

- **Determine the style combo of others:** What style combinations do you see in those you interact with the most?

- **Continue observing:** It sounds easy, but it requires deliberate attention.

STRATEGY 32:
Identify the Styles of Others

Now that you have an idea of the individual styles, their tendencies, and the varying combinations, it's time to learn how to identify someone's behavior style. Why? Because you live and work with people of different styles. Understanding that your spouse's Driver tendencies aren't a sign that he or she thinks you are lazy could help you a lot. Understanding that your Analytical coworker's need to study every possible outcome isn't something he does just to see your face turn purple and could also change the dynamics of your working relationship.

At the same time, it's important to remember that this is not a science, but an art that takes practice and patience.

I often joke that if you want to identify someone's style, watch how they manage breakfast. Drivers wouldn't bring in breakfast, so if someone brings breakfast, you know it wasn't a Driver. An Expressive would bring in donuts and send an email to everyone letting them know that they were the one who brought the donuts, and that they'll be in the break room if you want to stop by and say hello. Amiables want you to be cared for and fed, but they don't want attention, so they bring in the donuts, slip them into the breakroom, and quickly return to work. This works out perfectly for the Expressives who can now pretend that they were the ones who brought the donuts! Meanwhile, the Analytical is still at the donut shop determining the proper count, divided by the potential number of donut eaters, factoring in that some may be gluten- or dairy-intolerant.

Another approach to identifying someone's style is asking, "Tell me about yourself." Drivers typically begin with their job titles or what they do for a living. Expressives start from birth and work their way up to the present. Amiables will say, "I don't want to bore you with me. Tell me about you!" Analyticals will return with, "What do you want to know?"

Yet another approach would be to ask for directions. Drivers will send you a link to a Google map. Expressives will give you landmarks and have great stories about each one. Amiables will ask where you're coming from so they may give you the most convenient directions. Analyticals will use almost military navigation: Travel .2 miles heading northeast, then veer 45 degrees to the west.

Or you could just ask yourself these questions:

1. What is their pace? Are they fast-paced and impatient, or are they slow-paced and patient? Observe the way they talk, eat, manage tasks, and behave in general. Do they tend to be impatient and interrupt others (so they don't forget what they were going to say), or do they listen, process, and then respond?

2. What is their focus? Do they focus more on facts, tasks, and results, or do they focus more on people, emotions, and relationships? Are they looking at objective facts, deadlines, milestones, and using words like "I think," or are they focusing more on the people involved and using words like "I feel"?

The following style summary helps determine style. Start by identifying the individual's pace, followed by their focus.

If you are absolutely stuck and cannot figure out their pace or their focus, there's a strong likelihood that the person is fairly evenly distributed, making it hard to isolate a dominant style. It's much easier to identify someone's style if he or she has at least one high score.

STYLE SUMMARY

FACTS & RESULTS

Analytical	**Driver**
Analysis	Control
Logic-driven	Decisive
Non-emotional	Impatience
System and Process	Results-driven

SLOW & PATIENT ———————————— **FAST & IMPATIENT**

Amiable	**Expressive**
Adaptable	Communication
Loyal	Emotion-driven
No Conflict	Non-detailed
Relationship-driven	Recognition

PEOPLE & EMOTIONS

Now that you have an idea of the individual styles, their tendencies, and the varying combinations, it's time to learn how to identify someone's behavior style. Why? Because you live and work with people of different styles.

SLIGHT EDGE STRATEGY

- **Observe those around you:** Pay attention to the people with whom you interact most frequently. Are they fast-paced and impatient or slow-paced and impatient? Are they more focused on people and relationships or facts and results?

- **Think about your interactions:** Which styles are easier or more difficult for you to interact with? How do these interactions make you react?

- **Create a list:** Make a list of the important people in your life (family members, friends, boss, coworkers, etc.). What is their dominant style?

- **Ask the people you frequently interact with the following questions:**

  - What is the best way to communicate with you?

  - How do you like to receive positive feedback and constructive criticism?

  - What do you need to remain productive?

STRATEGY 33: Adapt Your Style

Once you've identified someone's style, you may flex and adapt your style to improve communication and results. This is where most people get hung up: "Why should I have to change who I am for them? Why don't they have to change?"

It's important to remember that you are not changing who you are. You are simply modifying the way you approach people. Think about the following statement:

If I understand me better than you understand you, I can guide the communication between us. If I understand me and you better than you understand yourself, I can actually predict and guide how you will respond.

What does that sound like to you? I'll give you a hint: it starts with the letter M. Some say manipulation, others say marriage. If I modify my approach so that I win at your expense, it is absolutely manipulation, and it's wrong. If, however, I approach you a certain way because I know you are more likely to be receptive and we both end up getting what we need, that is the goal of communication.

It goes back to the fundamental question I posed in Strategy 27: Is your goal to be right or to get it right? If you are truly trying to get it right, while it might require more work on your part, modifying the way you present the message is often the only way to achieve the desired result.

Should you always have to be the one to modify your style? Only if your true goal is to get it right. You only have control over what you do and how well you do it. Trying to change someone else is about as effective as trying to apply makeup while riding a bull. It just doesn't work—believe me, I've tried (changing people, not riding a bull and applying makeup).

There's a big difference between knowing how to do something and actually doing it. I've been practicing these skills for well over 15 years, and I have two degrees in communication, and I still don't always get it right. Unfortunately, knowing how to do something doesn't always translate into doing it. Flexing and adapting to others requires more than skill. It requires patience and a willingness to leave your comfort zone.

I find myself constantly having to adapt my style when dealing with Evan or with Rylee. Evan is very much a Driver, and he wants what he wants when he wants it. Rylee is highly Expressive and Analytical. We find her dancing around the house one minute and extremely frustrated the next because something in her room is out of place.

We all have our quirks and idiosyncrasies. When we're calm, rested, and in our natural environment, it still requires effort to flex our style, but it is certainly much easier. When we're stressed, tired or frustrated, it requires significantly more energy to modify and adapt to others' styles.

Adapting for Drivers

Evan's therapist repeatedly reminds us: "Once you've engaged in a power struggle, you've already lost." This is especially true with Drivers.

With Drivers, avoid statements that start with "I feel," "You always," "You never," and "I wish you would." Instead, use statements that appeal to their logical side, like "It makes sense…" or "It stands to reason…" Drivers prefer to be approached logically, and they are more concerned with the result and outcome than how you feel.

Give Drivers a sense of control by offering a couple of options that you can live with, and let them choose. Never verbally attack a Driver (they will attack back); rather, focus on the behavior or the task at hand.

A Driver's most valuable commodity is time, so respect it. Unless they specifically ask, they don't want to hear about your weekend, see your pictures, and hear about your dog or kids. It doesn't mean they don't care. It just means that they are focused on getting things done before they "waste" time socializing. Match their level of socialization. If you ask how they're doing, and they respond with, "fine," don't go into a whole lot of detail if they return the question.

Pay attention to a Driver's nonverbal communication. If they tap their feet, look at their watch, or read email while you're talking, chances are they are not engaged. Follow the Driver's 3B philosophy: Be bright. Be brief. Be gone.

Adapting for Expressives

Expressives thrive in environments that are friendly, light-hearted, and fun. They are more emotional and appreciate being able to share humor and receive positive feedback. Expressives are wounded by being left out. Take time to build relationships with them.

Expressives have a tendency to lose focus in discussions. I lovingly refer to it as chasing bunnies, which can be frustrating for others. One minute they are highly focused on the task at hand, and the next min- ute…*bunny!* They typically realize they do this, so it's all right to gently point them back to the issue at hand.

In a business setting, rather than getting frustrated at the Expres- sives' need to socialize, plan for it and schedule an extra five or 10 min- utes before or after your meeting for small talk.

Expressives often need to process aloud, so when they generate ideas or offer suggestions, it's really their way of thinking through the process. Before you begin working on a task or project, ensure that it is in fact a priority, and something they want addressed. The same holds true for Drivers.

If an Expressive does something to help or provide value, make sure you thank them. Feeling appreciated motivates Expressives.

Adapting for Amiables

Take time to build relationships with Amiables (just like you would with Expressives). Slow down, provide reassurance, and avoid confrontation. Amiables need time to process, so give them time to think, without plac- ing pressure or demands.

If you want an Amiable to contribute to a meeting or discussion involving several other people, send questions in advance to give them time to think and process and always give them time to make a decision.

Avoid putting Amiables on the spot. They don't like to be embar- rassed. Respect their need for privacy. Amiables won't necessarily tell you if you have said or done something to upset them, so pay attention to their nonverbal communication.

Help Amiables see the effects of their contributions and allow them to work as part of a larger team. Communicate frequently to ensure that expectations have been clearly defined and are understood.

Adapting for Analyticals

Analyticals need to question and understand things, so don't take it personally when they challenge information. Analyticals are goal- and results-oriented, so it is best to approach them in a direct, straightforward way.

Analyticals appreciate respect for their space and prefer to have time to process and think about things before making decisions. To ensure deadlines are met, set realistic milestones along the way and ensure progress is being made. Clearly define expectations and pay attention to details. If you are meeting with an Analytical, be on time and be prepared.

If you are trying to persuade an Analytical, it is best to use logic and objective information to demonstrate that you've looked at both sides of the issue. Take time to think of questions that the Analytical may ask ahead of time so that you are prepared.

Avoid becoming emotional or defensive when communicating with an Analytical. If they feel threatened, they are likely to become argumentative, so provide them the time and space they need to think through problems and challenges.

Adapting with Various Styles at Once

If you're sending a mass email, holding a meeting, or just dealing with several people at once, make an effort to modify a little for each style. For example, if you're sending an email, start with a soft introduction for Amiables and Expressives ("good morning, hope this finds you well"). Then provide bullet points and the main idea for Drivers. Attach more detailed information for the Analytical. End with more of a relationship-driven statement ("I appreciate your time, thanks for your help, look forward to hearing from you"). One size does not fit all. Try to incorporate both relationship- and result-focused communication.

When you are communicating with a mixture of styles, be deliberate and provide each with information or communication that takes into account differences in pace and focus. Provide the big picture, then support it with details. Stay focused on the agenda but allow time for rapport and relationship building.

You can't please all the people all the time, but you can please most of the people most of the time.

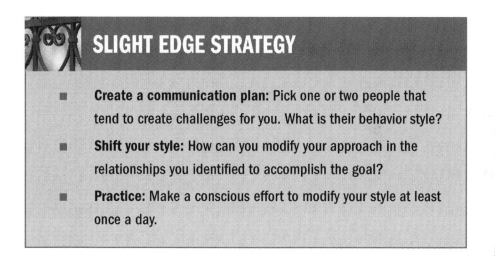

SLIGHT EDGE STRATEGY

- **Create a communication plan:** Pick one or two people that tend to create challenges for you. What is their behavior style?

- **Shift your style:** How can you modify your approach in the relationships you identified to accomplish the goal?

- **Practice:** Make a conscious effort to modify your style at least once a day.

STRATEGY 34: Defuse Difficult Situations

We talk about communication as our words, our gestures, and even our overall demeanor. All those things *are* communication. But there's a whole lot that goes on in our minds and hearts before our words or body language are ever revealed.

For example, into every communication we bring what we think and how we feel about ourselves. In fact, most of our communication is colored by how we feel about ourselves. If we see ourselves as victims or as superior to others, that will enter into our communication. We also bring what we think and feel about others, including prejudices, old triggers, and hot buttons. Every time we enter into a conversation about a project, decision, or agreement, we bring all of that with us. And so do the people we're talking to.

When you are frustrated by someone else's behavior, ask yourself how *you* might be contributing to the problem. What could you change about your mindset or approach that could make a difference? Remember, you have a lot more control over your own thoughts and behaviors than you do over anyone else's.

For example, although we don't like to think of it this way, we often train people to treat us the way they do. If someone makes unreasonable demands on us and we just give them what they ask for, we've signaled that that behavior is okay with us, so there's a good chance they will keep making unreasonable demands until we tell them it's not okay. Of course, we may be so frustrated by then that our communication comes out as anger. Since we've never complained about it before, our angry communication will make us look like the unreasonable ones. Review Strategy 30, where we talk about identifying the styles of others, so we can communicate our message to handle those difficult situations productively. Think about what attitudes and unspoken qualities we bring into a discussion.

- **Take your temperature:** The next time you get ready to enter a conversation that might be difficult, check your own "temperature." How do you feel about yourself right now? How do you feel about the person or people you're going to be interacting with? When you're emotional, being logical is not physiologically possible. You go into fight or flight mode, and this makes it virtually impossible to think and act rationally. If you are feeling upset or emotional, see if you can revisit the discussion when you've had time to calm down. If you're engaged in conversation and you see the other person is getting emotional, say something like, "Look, I know we want to work this out, but right now we're both pretty upset. Can we revisit this later today or tomorrow?"

- **Focus on the goal:** Before you enter the conversation, focus on the goal. What do you hope to get out of the conversation? What do you think the other person hopes to get out of it? People do things for one of two reasons: to experience pleasure or to avoid pain. If you take time to figure out what is in it for them, you have a much better chance of positively managing the relationship.

- **Ask questions:** Curiosity is one of the best strategies for minimizing uncertainty, defensiveness, and miscommunication. Ask questions with the intention of trying to understand, not just for the sake of asking. Lots of people don't ask questions because they don't want to be embarrassed or appear foolish. Just like my teacher always said, the only dumb questions are the ones never asked.

- **Really listen:** Asking questions makes it clear that you are interested in the other person's perspective, but then you must *listen!* The moment people see you are trying to understand them, they become less defensive. Rather than spending your time trying to convince someone that you are right, truly listen to understand where the other person is coming from. Listening is not an easy skill. It requires you to stop thinking and doing so that you are able to truly focus on what the other person is saying. You will be far more effective if your intent is to listen to understand, not to be understood.

- **Pay attention to your nonverbal communication:** The way we say something is often far more important than what we actually say. Although this certainly sounds like common sense, it's definitely not common practice. If we want results, we have to be conscious about the way we communicate and the way we are perceived.

  Most communication is nonverbal. People read your facial expressions, body language, and your overall demeanor, not to mention your rate of speech, pitch, and volume. When your verbal and nonverbal communications contradict each other, people believe the nonverbal. You can test this next time you ask someone who seems to be having a really bad day how they're doing. When they say, "I'm fine," do you believe them?

- **Q-TIP (Quit Taking It Personally):** Sometimes we think that the other person's behavior or tone is all about us. They could have all kinds of issues—a fight with their spouse, insecurity about their relationship to the boss, a bad morning with the kids—that affect show they communicate. Try to take a step back and depersonalize the situation. Chances are, it really isn't about you.

SLIGHT EDGE STRATEGY

- **Think about how you feel:** Before you go into a difficult conversation, check your "temperature." What are your feelings about yourself, the other person, and the purpose of the conversation? Are you thinking about battle or are you coming in with an open mind, ready to listen?

- **Improve your communication:** Most people resort to combat when they no longer have the skills to logically discuss the issue. What can you do to improve your communication skills so that you don't get caught in a negative cycle?

STRATEGY 35: Embrace Conflict

In Strategy 27, we talked about ways to get our minds in the right place before a difficult encounter. Another important consideration is facing our fear of conflict. Conflict terrifies a lot of us. Some of us were raised in a family where overt conflict wasn't allowed and we were passive-aggressive instead. Others were raised in a situation where really negative conflict—screaming and fighting—happened all the time, and we go to extraordinary lengths to avoid it. Neither is a healthy approach.

Conflict is crucial to healthy relationships and can produce more creative solutions and better outcomes, but only if it is handled correctly. Avoiding conflict until it boils up and explodes is not a healthy approach. Instead, we must learn to speak our minds and our needs in a constructive way. We must learn to communicate assertively.

Let's say, for example, that one of your triggers or hot buttons (more on those in Strategy 36) occurs when you're talking to someone, and they continue to check their email or look at their phone. You have a few choices when it comes to communicating how you're feeling:

- **Aggressive communication:** "You're not listening to me!"

- **Passive-aggressive communication:** Ignore it or say, "It's fine," when it's really not fine.

- **Assertive communication:** "Would you prefer we talk at a different time? It's hard for me to concentrate while you're on your phone," or "When you look at your phone when we're talking, I don't feel like I have your full attention."

With aggressive communication, you're forcing your anger on the other person. That's not an effective approach. In the second example, you're treating your own feelings as unimportant, which builds resentment. In the last scenario, you're honestly, but not angrily, communicating how you feel about the situation. That doesn't mean the other person will handle it well—many people don't like being called on their rude behavior no matter how nicely you try to do it—but you will have behaved like a mature adult.

There are other ways to communicate about difficult situations that are equally unproductive and unhelpful. Let's say your boss asks you to do a task you don't have time to do. You could say one of two things:

- "I'm already completely overloaded and stressed. I just can't do it."

- "Sure. I have a list of projects that I'm working on. Let me get it, and you can help me determine where this task should go in order of priority."

The first communication is a complaining, victim mentality, and is negative. The other is positive and solution-oriented, and involves the supervisor in helping to determine task priorities.

If communication is about being honest and seeking solutions, it has very different results from communication that's about venting concealed feelings or advancing hidden agendas like "my boss expects too much of me."

Get Rid of "You" Statements

Next, take "you" out of your language. Think about how you feel when someone begins with "You should" or "You always." Instantly, we become defensive. When someone begins a sentence with "I feel" or "I need," you are generally more receptive.

Of course, the best case scenario is to depersonalize the statement all together.

Rather than saying, "You aren't listening to me," try "Please let me finish what I was saying."

Or instead of, "You said you would finish this by today," try "The project really needs to be finished today. What do we need to do to make that happen?"

If that doesn't work, try this formula: "When you _____, it makes me feel _____. In the future, it would help if we could _____." This works particularly well with Expressives and Amiables. With Drivers and Analyticals, remember to focus on results.

Get Curious

Ask questions, empathize, and paraphrase. Use statements like, "I want to make sure I understand where you're coming from. What I hear you saying is…" If you have missed the mark, or if they have misstated their perspective, this gives you both a chance for a do-over, while allowing you both to keep your dignity. That keeps the misunderstanding small, rather than having it grow into a conflict or launching into a project where you really don't have agreement. When you ask questions and paraphrase, it demonstrates that you really care about understanding them. Remember, listen to understand, not to be understood.

SLIGHT EDGE STRATEGY

- **Reflect on how you communicate:** Spend some time this week reflecting on communication patterns you may have during arguments or heated discussions that produce less than favorable results. Do you start sentences with an accusatory "you"? Do you really try to find out what the other person is saying, or are you just waiting for the other person to finish speaking so you can get your point across?

- **Practice assertive communication:** Practice asserting yourself in low-risk situations (preferably with people who will love you anyway, even if you screw it up).

- **Ask questions:** Get curious. Paraphrase. Do this as often as possible.

STRATEGY 36: Beware of Hot Buttons

Before Evan was able to speak, he was able to argue. Part of his diagnosis is oppositional defiant disorder, which is a pattern of disobedient, hostile, and defiant behavior toward authority figures. Fun huh? In other words, I say up, Evan says down. I say dry, Evan says wet. I say it's time to get up for school, and Evan says I'm going to kill you. Since he was 11 months old, I've been working with therapists, both for him and me, to learn how to better manage his oppositionality.

If I were laid back and easygoing, it would make my life a whole lot easier. Unfortunately, those aren't exactly the words I would use to describe my personality.

Evan's therapist pointed out that once I entered a power struggle with him I had already lost. I began to see how that applied to all of my relationships. At one point in resolving a problem or reaching a decision, we might be exploring options, listening to each other's perspectives, considering compromises. But once we hit that place where we're just repeating the same idea in a louder voice or attacking the other person's perspective, we're in a power struggle and we are most likely trying to be right rather than get it right. Remember Strategy 27?

When we engage in a power struggle, our defenses go up, emotion takes over, and rational thought flies out the window. So how do we stop a power struggle, or better yet, avoid it altogether? Our family came up with a phrase: "Don't push the argue button."

When we can see that a conversation is starting to elevate our voices and heartbeats, that winning becomes key and being right is more important than getting it right, we know we're hovering over the argue button. Then it's time to either walk away, cool down, or shift our approach to one that's more focused on resolution.

I'm not suggesting that you should avoid conflict. Conflict is a healthy and necessary part of relationships, both personally and professionally. Extensive research has demonstrated that conflict, when managed properly, strengthens relationships and teams, and can serve as a catalyst for better solutions, innovation, and growth. But conflict has to be constructive, with people working to understand each other and find solutions, not just to win. And in some debates, nobody's likely to shift position. Often the issue isn't that important to either of our lives, so we should just walk away and go work, watch a movie, or take a walk instead. Sometimes we have to agree to disagree.

Rylee and I were debating something, where I was 100 percent convinced I was right. So was she. I said, "Honey, I think we're going to have to agree to disagree on this one." She replied, "Ok, as long as you know I'm right!"

Know Your Hot Buttons

One of the toughest and most crucial keys to managing conflict is to know our own hot buttons. Hot buttons are the triggers, words, phrases, facial expressions, or comments that make our blood boil. We might not even realize on a conscious level that it *is* a hot button, or *why* it makes our blood boil. All we know is that whenever someone does it, we go from being reasonable and goodhearted to angry, bitter, and frustrated in a matter of seconds. That's why it's called a hot button. Our kids seem to know all about our hot buttons, and some seem to push them on purpose just for the hell of it. I remember when I was growing up, the one that killed my mother was "what*ever*" and its accompanying eye roll. My kids are now paying me back, big time.

By having some self-awareness and communicating expectations to the people closest to us, we can minimize (not eliminate) the number of times our hot buttons get pushed, and we can spend less time reacting.

Pay attention to conversations, situations, or people who bother you. What is it about what they are saying, how they are saying it, or what they are doing that is causing frustration? What do you feel when the button is pushed, besides angry? With my mother, for example, I would guess that she felt dismissed and disrespected. That would probably be enough to frustrate anyone.

Although people we love will often work to avoid our hot buttons, we are only allowed so many free passes before we're labeled "high-maintenance." We shouldn't make people feel like they're walking through a minefield of hot buttons just to figure out what's for dinner. Some of our hot buttons—like "my ex used to do that"—are a personal issue and something we need to work out for ourselves.

You can also ask people close to you what their hot buttons are. You might be pushing hot buttons without even knowing it.

And keep in mind, arguing is exhausting and usually leaves both people feeling bad, grumpy, and spent. Think back on the arguments you've gotten into. Were they worth it? After all, we only have a certain amount of energy to spend, and just like time, we can't get it back once it's gone. Although I'm still guilty of getting sucked into arguments and power struggles now and then, I have found that having a simple phrase like "don't push the argue button" and knowing what my hot buttons are can be extremely helpful.

SLIGHT EDGE STRATEGY

- **List your hot buttons:** What are your hot buttons?

- **Determine your triggers:** What people or situations cause you to engage in power struggles? Who presses your hot buttons most often?

- **Identify the hot buttons of those around you:** What are the hot buttons of the people closest to you? How can you avoid pushing them?

STRATEGY 37:
Give the Benefit of the Doubt

Have you ever seen someone run a red light or a stop sign? What did you think about that person? Perhaps gems like, "Dumbass!" or "Where are the cops when you need them?" or "I can't believe they are so careless!" Now turn the tables. Have you ever accidentally run a red light or stop sign? If you have, what were you thinking after it happened? Maybe, "Oops!" or "I can't believe I just missed that!" or "I hope the cops didn't see!" What's different between someone else running a stop sign and you doing it? When you are the one at fault, you know your intent was not to harm others, but that you simply made a mistake. However, when someone else is at fault, you may be quick to judge, focusing on their behavior, and perhaps even assigning their poor actions to their character.

Why do we attribute our behavior to our intent or a simple accident and others' behaviors to the type of person they are? Why, when we have a bad morning, do we justify our irritability, yet when others are irritable we consider them difficult? Because we're human. Regardless of our intentions, people only know what they see through our actions, and we only know what we see through the actions of others. In between our intentions and our actions lies a chasm.

In early 2012, I was driving home from a client's office on a busy road, and a man cut me off, almost causing an accident. I was shaken, and I was pissed. What a careless driver. What a jerk. I immediately judged him and the type of person I thought him to be.

Fast forward to July 2013. I was headed home during rush hour when I received a frantic phone call from a good Samaritan—a nurse—who had witnessed an accident. She told me a man riding a motorcycle had been rear-ended on the freeway, flipped over his handle bars, and hit the car in front of him. He was barely conscious but asked her to call the most recent number dialed on his phone. That number was mine, and the motorcyclist was Jay. I panicked and drove like a lunatic toward the hospital.

I sped along the shoulder of the road, cut off cars, and got honked at and yelled at by the people I passed. I was scared and my only thought was to get to Jay at the hospital, consequences be damned.

I ended up beating the ambulance to the hospital, and I promptly melted down. How many laws had I broken to get there? How many lives had I inadvertently endangered? A bunch. Only I knew the situation and my only intention was to get to Jay. It was never my intention to be reckless. After a nerve-wracking hour of waiting, I finally saw Jay, alive and well, all things considered. He had been wearing all of his safety gear, and had only suffered eight broken ribs. Certainly no walk in the park, but he would be okay.

To all of the people I sped past, I was that horrible, reckless, and careless driver.

When push comes to shove, we are all doing the best we can with what we have at any given time. We are flawed, and we make mistakes.

You never know what's going on in someone else's life. Maybe they just lost a loved one or are going through a divorce. Maybe they are caring for a sick child or worried about making enough money to keep the electricity on. When someone behaves in a way inconsistent with our expectations, we usually make harsh judgments, are very quick to assign it as a character flaw, and form impressions that aren't usually very nice.

How do you give yourself and others the benefit of the doubt? How do you bridge the gap between intentions and actions? Try the following strategies:

1. **Pay attention:** As you go through your day, pay attention to the things you say and do. Are your actions aligned with your intentions? You might have the very best intentions, but are the choices you are making supporting them?

2. **Be deliberate:** Make a concerted effort to think about what you do and say before you do it and say it. How might it be perceived? Is the message you are trying to send the one being received?

3. **Hold off on judgment:** The next time someone does or says something that bothers you, take a few minutes to evaluate the situation logically. More often than not, the intent behind the message was positive, even if the action didn't appear that way.

4. **Give yourself and others a break:** We are all doing the best we can with what we have, and we are all struggling to manage the incredible amount of things we have going on, both personally and professionally.

5. **Be careful what you look for; you may find it:** If you are looking for all the reasons someone is difficult, or if you are searching to find negative intentions, that's what you'll most likely find. Instead, focus on the positive and give people the benefit of the doubt. You'll be amazed at how much good you see.

6. **Be self-aware:** As you go through your week, pay attention to your actions and how they might be perceived by others. Remember, people will judge you by your actions, not by your intentions.

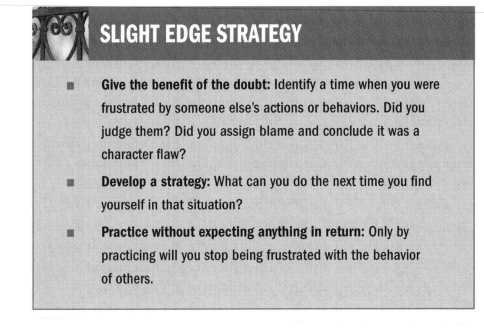

SLIGHT EDGE STRATEGY

- **Give the benefit of the doubt:** Identify a time when you were frustrated by someone else's actions or behaviors. Did you judge them? Did you assign blame and conclude it was a character flaw?

- **Develop a strategy:** What can you do the next time you find yourself in that situation?

- **Practice without expecting anything in return:** Only by practicing will you stop being frustrated with the behavior of others.

Part Three:

LIFE LOVE & WORK

STRATEGY 38:
Forget the Idea of Balance

I'm just going to say it: The concept of a balanced life is bullshit. There, I feel better.

Let's look at modern life for a minute. On an average day, we are bombarded with thousands of images and hundreds of thousands of pieces of new information. We hold all of this information in our subconscious. In reality, our short-term memory can only store two to four items at once. When we are feeling overwhelmed or stressed, it's not necessarily because we have so much to do; it's trying to remember it all and keep it at the forefront of our minds.

Likewise, this never-ending deluge of information and our constant need to stay connected is rendering us less social, preventing us from staying focused on any one thing for any length of time, and making us less productive.[18] How can we begin to focus on the conversation or task at hand with all that pinging, beeping, and buzzing distracting us?

So we're overwhelmed, we're distracted, and on top of that, we're getting hooked on this lifestyle. Most of us are in a constant state of adrenaline overload. The hormone adrenaline was meant to give us short bursts of energy to go after food or escape a predator. In modern life, we get this intense adrenaline reaction with work, personal problems, emotional conflict, even traffic. This creates stress and, ironically, we have become addicted to that stress. In *The Power of Full Engagement*,[19] authors Jim Loehr and Tony Schwartz explain that people who operate at high levels

---

[18]Kendra Cherry, "Multitasking: The Cognitive Costs of Multitasking," about.com/psychology, available at http://psychology.about.com/od/cognitivepsychology/a/costs-of-multitasking.htm.

[19]Jim Loehr and Tony Schwartz, *The Power of Full Engagement: Managing Energy, Not Time, Is the Key to High Performance and Personal Renewal* (New York: The Free Press, 2003).

of intensity for long periods can actually get addicted to the "high" you get from adrenaline, noradrenaline, and cortisol.

Like many other drugs, adrenaline and stress are making us sick. According to the American Academy of Family Physicians, two-thirds of all office visits to family physicians are due to stress-related symptoms.[20] Some doctors believe that all illness is stress-induced. Stress is linked to the six leading causes of death: heart disease, cancer, lung ailments, accidents, cirrhosis of the liver, and suicide.

In the midst of this information overload, endless tasks, and unhealthy addiction to stress, we're somehow supposed to balance our lives. What does that even look like? Work on one side and Zen-like relaxation on the other?

The Simple Truth

As the mother (and once single mother) of a special needs child, a business owner, friend, daughter, volunteer, etc., I can tell you, emphatically, that there is absolutely no such thing as balance. We are making ourselves crazy trying to find it, and it's a mirage.

I think the major flaw in our search for balance is that our lives are not supposed to be balanced.

The idea of work-life balance was first introduced in the eighteenth and nineteenth centuries. It was a different time, and the concept was intended to prevent laborers from having to work 16 hours a day, six days a week. If you are working that much, it might be time to consider a career change, or at the very least a serious mindset shift.

As we have changed as a culture, the idea of work-life balance is a little less clear. Can you be the executive who thrives at business, the mother who volunteers at her child's school, the friend who maintains an active social life, and yet still remain sexy, fit, and fun? Maybe for a short time, but it certainly isn't sustainable.

Come on, get real. We are all doing the best we can with what we've got. You might be great at doing each of these things on different days, and you may even have some days where you manage to do it all—but no one can consistently balance everything flawlessly.

---

[20]Human Sustainability Institute, *Stress Statistics* (2011), available at www.humansustainability institute.com.

BALANCE WHEEL

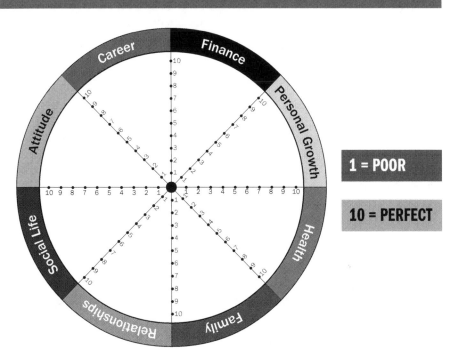

1 = POOR

10 = PERFECT

There are some things that should take precedence over others. These things are called our priorities, and we can only focus on one priority at a time.

Trying to juggle Evan, work, doctors, friends, Jay, Rylee, volunteer work, my health, and my sanity is not easy. I struggle just like everyone else, and I have figured some things out along the way.

First of all, start with where you are. On the Balance Wheel above, rate yourself by drawing a dot on the corresponding line that represents where you currently feel you are in each category (with 1 being poor and 10 being perfect).

Next, set priorities. Identify the areas of your life that really matter and prioritize them. Your goal isn't necessarily going from a 2 to 10. The goal is making Slight Edge changes, like going from a 2 to a 4. Schedule time for your priorities. If necessary, save money for them. Make sure you have emotional and physical energy for them.

Don't try to multitask while you're prioritizing. Be where you are when you're there. Identify your top three to five priorities and spend 80 percent of your time on them without apologizing for it. Most of us have gotten pretty adept at prioritizing our schedule. Scheduling our priorities should be our real goal.

Be honest with yourself. Of course we would like to think we value relationships more than money, and family more than work. But do we really? When push comes to shove, do your actions support your real priorities? In other words, do your actions match your intentions?

There are lots of tools and tips for managing the onslaught of information and tasks we have to deal with. One of the most important is just making sure that the priorities in your life aren't passing by while you're reacting in stress mode. There's no such thing as balance. As long as the bulk of your attention is on what's really important, that's okay.

SLIGHT EDGE STRATEGY

- **Create and fill out your Balance Wheel:** You can use the one provided or make your own. Feel free to create your own categories. You can have as few as two or as many as 20—however many you need to illustrate your own life situation.

- **Be honest with yourself:** Re-evaluate your answers with brutal honesty to see if the things you're claiming as your priorities are really getting priority attention.

- **Prioritize:** Make sure you carve out ample time for the things that are most important. Focus on them without multitasking so that you're giving them your full attention.

STRATEGY 39: Find Your WIIFM

We all want to motivate someone. Wives complain about motivating their husbands. Parents struggle to motivate their kids to get good grades or clean up their rooms. Organizations try all the time to come up with something that will motivate employees, from a company coffee mug to bonuses or a cushy parking space. In reality, no one can inject motivation into someone else (most of us have tried and failed), and our efforts fall far short of our goal.

Why? Because people have different motivators. One person is motivated most by the opportunity to contribute whereas another is motivated by having the freedom to choose how to contribute. The bottom line is WIIFM: What's In It For Me? It's the secret to motivation and it's not selfish.

People already have desires. They want respect, peace of mind, success, recognition, financial stability, admiration, love—all kinds of things. Those are the things that motivate them to work harder, take risks, and change behaviors. The truth about motivation: You can't actually motivate another person. The closest you can get is to figure out what already motivates them and tap into it.

Which Works Better? The Carrot or the Stick?

There are also negative motivators, fear being chief among them: fear of failure, fear of loss of respect, fear of loss of love or money. Some people are able to motivate others in the short-term by stimulating those fear motivators. It never lasts, and it never produces the best results.

Let's not forget incentives as a motivator. We all love that $10 gift card to Target. Unfortunately once we get an incentive, we crave more. Eventually, we feel entitled.

Many of us have very rudimentary and dated ideas about motivation. The poster child for motivation is a donkey pulling a cart with rocks in it, with a carrot dangling off a stick hanging in front of his head. This looks simple, right? If the donkey wants the carrot, he'll pull the cart. But what has to be true for this to work? The donkey has to be hungry. He has to like carrots. He has to think he can get the carrot. Once he gets it, he eats, gets full, and you have to wait for him to get hungry again. Next time, you have to give him two carrots, or some strawberries, or lighten the load. If all else fails, you take the carrot off the stick and whack the donkey with it. But this is the old way of "motivating others," and the approaches most people try first are seldom the most effective.

Motivation, by itself, is neither good nor bad. You can be motivated to work hard, or you can be motivated to steal a car. Motivating other people isn't inherently good or bad either. If I use tactics to motivate you to do something that will only benefit me and be costly to you, that's manipulation. However, if I know what motivates you, and I use that to help us both achieve our goal, that's effective communication and influence. If I can help you find your inner motivation and it benefits us both, then we both win.

Which brings us to the crux of the issue: Helping someone find the inner motivation to do something is really about personal leadership and influence. The true question is not, "How can I motivate someone?" A better question to ask is, "How do I create a climate that taps into what already motivates this person?"

Whatever situation you're in, at work or at home, you're more likely to get what you need and have win-win outcomes if you are able to understand both your motivators and the motivators of others. If you want to create an environment where people want to help you and do things for you, you have to find out what drives their behavior.

How do you find out people's WIIFM? Try these strategies:

1. **Pay attention:** If you pay attention to what people talk about, what they are interested in, and what they focus on, you can often get a sense of what naturally motivates them.

2.   **Ask:** It may seem fairly simple, but when was the last time you asked people what you could do to help them stay motivated?

3.   **Figure out what de-motivates someone and stop doing it!** It's not rocket science. If you know someone hates to be nagged, talk to them about the way they would like to be approached when there are things to do. If you know that someone gets embarrassed easily, make a concerted effort not to put them in uncomfortable situations.

What's Your WIIFM?

Do you know what motivates you? If not, spend some time thinking about it. Then tap into it. You are the only person who can keep you motivated. Waiting for your spouse, kids, boss, employees, friends, or family to motivate you is a recipe for disappointment. You know yourself better than anyone.

At one of his speaking events, someone challenged motivational speaker Zig Ziglar: "Zig, motivation just doesn't last!" Good ol' Zig said, "Neither does bathing. That's why I recommend it daily."

Someone once asked me "How do you stay so motivated all the time?" I was taken aback. My response was simply, "What makes you think I'm motivated all the time?" For a motivational speaker, it's a good reputation to have, but trust me, I have to work at it every day.

Motivation isn't a magical formula. I wish there was a secret recipe where I could add a dash of this and a splash of that and boom!—instant motivation. Unfortunately, it just doesn't work like that. Motivation, just like anything else, requires effort.

Too many people wait around until something or someone mysteriously motivates them. Unfortunately or fortunately, depending on how you look at it, no one can make you motivated. Although people or events can certainly give you a push in the right direction, true motivation has to come from within.

You can't light a spark in others until one is lit in you. In the quest to influence and motivate, it begins with you.

SLIGHT EDGE STRATEGY

- **Make a list:** Create a list with two columns—one for your primary motivators and one for your primary de-motivators.

- **Make another list:** Write a list of the primary motivators and de-motivators of key people in your life. (If you don't know what they are, it doesn't hurt to ask.)

- **Create a strategy:** Strategize some ways you can begin adjusting your behavior to work within the motivators and de-motivators you've identified.

STRATEGY 40: Be Productive

We travel at warp speed so much of the time, it's often difficult to stop long enough to really ponder where it is we are trying to go. Frequently we mistake being very busy with being very productive, and they are not the same.

When I started consulting, I was extremely busy. I was busier than I'd ever been. I also worked for more than six months before I made a single dime, and it was my fault. When I stopped and looked at how I was spending my time, my typical day consisted of coffee and networking meetings, reading or attending a training session or workshop, researching the latest and greatest on organizational development, and building training workshops and presentations. There's one little thing missing on this list that is fundamental to being an effective consultant—clients. I wasn't selling. It never occurred to me that I had to actually go out and sell this stuff. I stopped cold in my tracks and identified my high-payoff activities. This is the best way to stop being busy and start being productive.

A high-payoff activity is an activity that brings the greatest result for the time invested. It is another version of the Pareto Principle. The Pareto Principle is the rule of 80/20: 20 percent of X, creates 80 percent of Y. For example, 20 percent of the employees do 80 percent of the work. Twenty percent of the customers generate 80 percent of the business. Twenty percent of the tasks that we do on any given day generate 80 percent of our results. These are our high-payoff activities (HPAs). These are not always the most enjoyable activities, and they aren't always the ones we would choose to do, but they do generate results. For some, it is making or taking phone calls. For others it is sales, completing paperwork, creating a product, or providing a service. These activities may shift and change over time, but in essence, they are the tasks and responsibilities of our jobs that bring us the greatest return for time invested. The focused planning and prioritizing of our HPAs will provide huge dividends.

Many of us have never identified our HPAs. We might focus on the thing that's the most enjoyable or even the thing that keeps our bosses off our backs, but those aren't necessarily our high-payoff activities.

What is an activity that you do at work that is the reason your job exists? What are a few tasks that, if you stopped doing them, the company would have to scramble to figure out a way to get them done? Which tasks create the highest revenue return or the highest productivity return? Identify the one thing that, if you did nothing else, would need to get done, then the second, third, etc.

Create a list of the top five or six things you think are your HPAs. Once you have your list, ask your supervisor or manager to jot down what he or she perceives to be your top five or six HPAs. Then compare lists. One of two things will happen:

1. **You will either validate that you are investing the right energy on the right things.**

   Or

2. **You will identify that your perceptions are different from that of your manager.**

Either outcome provides an opportunity to clarify expectations and goals. Are your HPAs tasks and responsibilities that allow you to focus on your strengths? If not, what can you do to spend more time focused on the things you enjoy? No one likes doing things that are difficult for them; for the most part, we enjoy tasks that capitalize on our strengths. If your HPAs don't align with your strengths, what are one or two things you could do to refocus your time and energy? What can you do every day to focus on your HPAs?

I realized very quickly that my top high-payoff activities, other than planning and prioritizing my day, were sales and speaking events. Both brought me paychecks and new clients. Networking over coffee and gleaning more education were great, too, but my business was getting paid to share my knowledge and expertise, not just spend all my time collecting more. Sales and speaking became daily goals, and I devoted time, energy, and effort to ensure they happened.

Jay and I also use this concept at home. We write down what we think are our relationship high-payoff activities and our family high-payoff activities. Agreeing on our HPAs allows us to better figure out how to mutually invest our time.

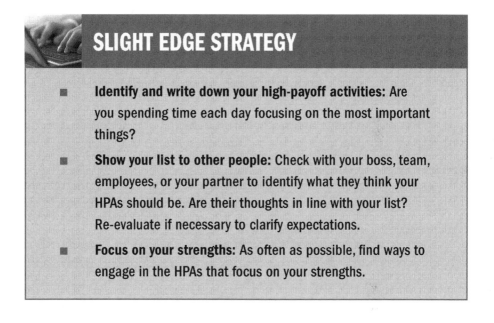

SLIGHT EDGE STRATEGY

- **Identify and write down your high-payoff activities:** Are you spending time each day focusing on the most important things?

- **Show your list to other people:** Check with your boss, team, employees, or your partner to identify what they think your HPAs should be. Are their thoughts in line with your list? Re-evaluate if necessary to clarify expectations.

- **Focus on your strengths:** As often as possible, find ways to engage in the HPAs that focus on your strengths.

STRATEGY 41: Develop SMART Goals

like to think of goals as a road map. When I am going to drive somewhere new, I look to Google maps to get directions. Once I provide my starting location and destination, Google magically provides several different route options. It's up to me to figure out which one I want to take to get from Point A to Point B.

Do I want to take the fastest route or the scenic route? Which route will cost me more money? Which route avoids congested traffic? Which route keeps me farthest from having to visit obnoxious Aunt Ida? If I'm driving with my family, what are their needs and priorities going to be? Almost any goal I set for myself will include bringing them along, and if they're not traveling cheerfully, it's going to be a long, hard road.

Let's say one of the goals on your dream board (see Strategy 7 if you need a refresher on creating your own dream board) is to be really physically fit. You decide the way to get there is to lose 30 pounds and exercise for 45 minutes five days a week. If you're starting out at Point A and eating nothing but comfort food and exercising zero minutes zero days a week, then you're essentially looking at a road trip from New York to Los Angeles. How do you get there? By setting goals and identifying action steps to accomplish them.

SMART Goals

In my work and in my life, I've studied the whole goal-setting process from every angle, and I believe firmly in SMART goals: Specific, Measurable, Attainable, Relevant, and Time Bound.

It works like this: Your dream board illustrates a really fit and healthy vision of you. Now you need to write down a SMART goal to get there.

- What is your goal? How are you going to measure it? Is it doable? How much time are you giving yourself to accomplish it?

- What benefit are you going to achieve, or what loss you will avoid by accomplishing this goal? This is your personal motivation, and what keeps you going when things get rough.

- What obstacles are you likely to face when you try to achieve this goal? You know they're going to be there. Plot strategies for overcoming the obstacles. The strategies have to be things that make it easier—not more complicated—to reach your goal.

- What are you going to do on a daily basis to achieve that goal? Write it down and post it where you can see it. One study I read about revealed that Harvard MBA graduate students who wrote down their goals earned on average 10 times more than those who had no written goals.[21]

This is planning your road trip. Let's say your goal for the first month is to lose five pounds and start exercising 30 minutes three days a week. Your Goal Planning Sheet (see Strategy 42 for a blank one) might look like this.

Goal: I will lose five pounds by March 15!

- **Benefits:** Clothes will fit better. It will be less stressful to get dressed in the morning because I won't freak out looking for something I can close over my gut. I will feel happier with myself and probably be more successful since I'm more outgoing and confident when I feel good about myself. I will be healthier and closer to the goal on my dream board.

- **Loss to Be Avoided:** Buying new clothes in a larger size. Wasting time getting dressed. Health risks associated with being overweight, stressed out, and unhappy. Heart disease, diabetes, joint

---

[21] Ashley Feinstein, "Why You Should Be Writing Down Your Goals," *Forbes* (April 8, 2014), available at www.forbes.com.

pains, other problems associated with excess weight. Missing opportunities because I'm feeling unattractive and more closed off.

- **Possible Obstacles:** I don't have time to work out. I travel a lot. I sit at a desk all day. It's hard to plan healthy meals. I'm tired in the evening and don't want to cook. I love treats and hate to deny myself.

- **Possible Solutions:** I can plan the week's meals on the weekend and shop in advance for ingredients. I can pick meals that don't take long to prepare or can be prepared in advance. I can stand and work part of the time. I can choose healthy meals and snacks while traveling. I can get low-fat, low-sugar, low-carb treats.

- **Action Steps:** Get up 30 minutes earlier so I have time to work out each morning. Choose healthy foods and plan meals ahead. Track calories I'm eating in a free app. Weigh myself. Drink a lot of water. Don't shame myself! That leads to overeating.

This same system works with every kind of goal: saving money, getting a better job, being a better parent, spouse, child, friend, and so on. If we've been going the wrong way for some time, it certainly can be difficult. For some reason, when we're on a road trip and we realize we're going the wrong way, we immediately look for a place to turn around. In life, if we've been going the wrong way, we often just decide it's easier and less stressful to keep going the way we are and hope it all works out.

SLIGHT EDGE STRATEGY

- **Pick a goal:** What SMART goal do I want to work on this week?

- **Answer these questions:**

  - What are the benefits?

  - What are potential obstacles and solutions?

  - What action steps will I take?

STRATEGY 42: Rethink Goal Setting

When Evan was six, he stood over my bed one Saturday morning and said, "Mommy, get up or I'm gonna kick you in the asp." Ah, the love of a child.

The truth is we all need a little "kick in the asp" every once in a while. When it comes down to it, there are really only two reasons we don't accomplish our goals:

1.   We don't start.

2.   We don't finish.

Once you establish your priorities, it's time to set a few goals. What is needed is a process. Whether it's a big goal or a small one, we require a process to see it through. This is certainly not a new concept, but we make it so complex that it becomes daunting.

The first step is to write down your goal. Countless studies exist about how important this is. Statistics vary, but the bottom line is that you are most likely to achieve your goals if you write them down. It keeps you accountable to yourself and challenges you to crystallize your thinking.

In Strategy 41, I explained how to develop SMART goals. Remember, they're the tried and true method of goal setting—Specific, Measurable, Achievable, Relevant, and Time-Bound. Setting SMART goals is creating a map of exactly how you will achieve your goals. For now, pick a goal that you want to accomplish and simply write it down.

The second step toward achieving your goal is recalibrating the way you talk to yourself. For example, don't begin with "I want to." If your goal is to want to, you've already accomplished it. It must start with "I will" or "by X date, this goal will be accomplished." Now you might say, come on, does that really matter? Absolutely. We believe the messages we send ourselves, and we are very visual. The correct wording makes a huge difference.

Next, think about the things you say to yourself while you're working on your goal. I have had a bad habit of speaking to myself harshly: "I shouldn't have said that" or "I can't believe I ate that!" When we internalize messages like that, we reinforce negative ideas about ourselves that will actually hinder our success.

Here's another interesting fact. Our brains don't really register all the words we say. If you say things like, "I won't be unhealthy," your brain doesn't register the "won't." All you hear is "unhealthy." Try saying things in the present tense as if they are already true. I know it seems a bit odd at first, but you become what you repeatedly think and do. In other words, what you think about, you bring about. Change your messages so that they are in the present tense and positive. For example, "I am healthy and strong" or "I live life to the fullest."

We believe one person more than anyone in the world. This person is so powerful that he or she will determine whether or not you succeed. Who is this person? You are!

The third step is critical and requires a lot of practice. After you've written down the statements you've created, put them in places where you will see them constantly. Look at them, read them, learn from them. If you don't want to do that, get a visual reminder. Just remember, out of sight, out of mind.

As you go through your goal-setting process, keep in mind these questions:

- What are my personal and professional goals?

- Where do I currently stand and where do I want to be?

- What is my plan to reduce the gap?

- What is my WIIFM (What's In It For Me)? You must have a strong personal motivator.

- What resources will I need?

- How will I track and manage my success?

- How will I reward myself?

- What are the benefits to be gained by accomplishing the goal?

- What are potential obstacles that could get in my way?

- What are possible solutions to those obstacles?

- What small, manageable action steps will I take each day, week, month, etc.?

- How will I plan and prioritize daily and incorporate my action steps into my daily routine?

- How will I celebrate my success?

- If I get off track, how do I make sure I don't completely derail?

Use the following Goal Planning Sheet to practice focusing on one goal. Remember Slight Edge. You don't have to set 10 goals, just one. When you accomplish it, move on to the next.

GOAL PLANNING SHEET

SMART Goal (Specific, Measurable, Attainable, Realistic, Time Bound):

_____

_____

_____

_____

_____

What's in it for me?:

_____

_____

_____

_____

_____

Possible Obstacles   Possible Solutions

_____   _____

_____   _____

_____   _____

_____   _____

_____   _____

Priority	Specific Action Step for Achieving This Goal	Target Date	Date Completed

SLIGHT EDGE STRATEGY

- **Revisit the Balance Wheel:** Flip to the Balance Wheel you completed in Strategy 38. Identify one area you would like to improve.

- **Develop one SMART Goal:** Use the Goal Planning Sheet to set one goal to be completed this week. Refer to Strategy 41 for more on setting your personal and professional goals.

- **Track your progress:** What will you need to do each day to achieve the goal by the end of the week?

- **Celebrate your success!**

STRATEGY 43: Plug the Leaks

Wwe talk a lot about "time management": finding ways to plug all those little leaks where we're interrupted, our minds drifts, or we're endlessly doing tasks that really don't matter. But we can't actually manage time. What we can manage is our focus, our attention, our energy. That's how we become more productive. Unfortunately, there are all kinds of gremlins that arise when we're trying to be productive, and they can steal our enjoyment of our work and our success.

Over the years, I've found that the following strategies are particularly helpful in managing energy, focus, attention, and productivity.

Do a Brain Dump

We cannot keep nearly as much information in the forefront of our minds as we think we can. That's how we get overwhelmed, distracted, and forget things. Once a day, make sure you do a brain dump. Get everything out of your head and onto a piece of paper or into a document. Write things down as you think of them, and devote five or 10 minutes a day to getting it out of your head and onto paper.

Manage Interruptions

Time is one of the only things we can't buy, manufacture, or win. It can certainly be wasted, and if we don't guard it carefully, it can be snatched from us in the form of interruptions. We don't really think of interruptions necessarily as huge time wasters because they're often brief and we return to our tasks right away.

Do the math. It is estimated that each interruption wastes between 10 to 15 minutes, including time to re-engage in the task we were doing before we were interrupted. If we save 30 minutes a day being more productive—the time it takes for two or three interruptions—that is the equivalent of having an extra 22 days a year! Imagine what you could do with 22 days!

Who is the worst culprit when it comes to interruptions? You are. Drifting thoughts, multitasking, constantly checking email and texts, and staying glued to social media are your biggest time wasters. Turn off your new mail alert, turn off your technology, and do one thing at a time.

Managing interruptions from others is the next step. This is often difficult because you may have already trained friends, family, and coworkers that it's okay to interrupt you. If you want them to stop, you have to retrain them. For some of us, especially people pleasers, that's hard to do. You're worth your time, too. The world will not end if you let people know that every day, you need an hour or two of uninterrupted time. So how do you begin?

Remove the candy from your desk. It encourages drive-bys. Tell people that if they need something, unless it is an emergency, you can help them before or after the time you've carved out to be uninterrupted. Put your phone on "do not disturb," close your door, or hang a sign on your cubicle. Try making a clipboard available so people can leave you a note.

Next, track your interruptions. Is it a certain person? If one person keeps coming back with questions, ideas, or pictures of his or her grandchildren, you'll need to make sure that person knows your boundaries and expectations. Suggest that they compile a list of questions or thoughts and bring them all to you once or twice a day.

Maybe there's a certain time of day when you are most often interrupted. You can make sure that time is dedicated to being available for questions, meetings, and discussions. Either way, be deliberate about the interruptions you allow. After all, it's your time. Would you give away your money to anyone who came in your office and asked for it? Treat your time the same way.

Eat Your Frog

Procrastination wastes energy and brain space. Putting off a task requires a lot of mental work and takes a tremendous amount of energy. Mark Twain once said, "If you eat a frog first thing in the morning, nothing else will seem that bad for the rest of the day." Entrepreneur and success expert Brian Tracey carried this idea further in his book, *Eat That Frog.*[22] So every morning, before you check your social media or read your emails, pick your most difficult task of the day—your frog—and get it done. If you can't eat the whole frog, set a timer for 30 minutes and eat a frog leg. Do as much as you can in 30 minutes and feel good about getting some of it done.

Take Control of Technology

Take control of technology, rather than letting it take control of you. I don't know why, but the "You've Got Mail" notification is like crack. As soon as we see it, we have to check. Why? If something is that urgent, email is not the best way to communicate. Turn off your email reminder. If you can, dedicate a couple of times a day to check email and return voicemails. Remember, you train people how to treat you. It doesn't mean you're not responsive. It means you have the ability to re-define what responsiveness looks like.

Keep Track of Time You're Saving

Don't forget to track your progress and celebrate success. For some reason, when we don't accomplish a goal we beat ourselves up, but when we accomplish a goal we're quick to gloss over our accomplishment or attribute it to luck. Work hard. Then reward yourself.

Remember the old saying, "How do you eat an elephant? One bite at a time." Think Slight Edge. The changes you make don't have to be drastic in order to get big results. Make minor adjustments in the way you live and work each day and be consistent.

---

[22] Brian Tracey, *Eat That Frog: 21 Great Ways to Stop Procrastinating and Get More Done in Less Time* (San Francisco: Berrett-Koehler, 2007).

SLIGHT EDGE STRATEGY

- **Pinpoint your biggest productivity leaks:** What are your biggest distractions or the things that keep you from being most productive?

- **Tackle one at a time:** Begin with the one that cuts most deeply into your productivity, like interruptions or managing email. Once you've conquered that, take on the next one.

- **Celebrate your success:** Even the little successes. You've earned it. Remember, strive for progress, not perfection.

STRATEGY 44: Cultivate Your Strengths

Once upon a time, a group of animals created a school for their children. There were ducks, frogs, birds, rabbits, fish, llamas, etc. The curriculum consisted of running, jumping, flying, and swimming. Each animal had to take all classes. For the purposes of this story, we'll follow Rodney Rabbit.

The first day of school was running class. Rodney Rabbit was fantastic! His teacher praised him and called his parents to let them know how well he had done in class. The second day was jumping class. Once again, Rodney excelled. He scored his second A+ and proudly went home to tell his parents. He loved school.

The third day was flying class. Rodney didn't do so well. He fell out of the tree and broke his little rabbit's foot. He was very disappointed in himself. His teacher reassured him but sent a note home to Mr. and Mrs. Rabbit letting them know the school was putting Rodney in remedial flying classes.

The fourth day was swimming class. Poor Rodney almost drowned. The teacher sent another note home explaining that because Rodney was already so good at running and jumping, they were removing him from those classes and having him focus all of his time and energy on flying and swimming. Those were the areas where he needed the most improvement.

Rodney was devastated. All he wanted to do was run and jump, and now his days were filled with falling out of trees and near drowning incidents. Finally, Rodney had enough. He became depressed, dropped out of school, and ran away from home. He eventually joined a rabbit gang, started dealing bunny smack, and continued to go downhill.

How many times do we have people in our lives who are wonderful runners and jumpers, yet we continually get frustrated with them when they can't fly or swim? This happens in both our personal and professional lives. Whether it is a team member that is not a good fit for a specific project, or a friend or family member that just can't seem to change the things you wish they would do more or less of, the rabbit phenomenon is a constant battle.

Sadly, we are most frustrated with ourselves for our inability to swim or fly.

Play on Your Strengths

We each have strengths and talents that come naturally to us and that we enjoy. It is interesting that most of us spend so much time trying to fix our weaknesses that we become burned out, frustrated, and mediocre.

I'm often reminded of this when I play online puzzle games with Rylee. What takes me five minutes to figure out (and is typically wrong), she is able to do in seconds. At first, I was really frustrated with myself. How is this so easy for her, yet so difficult for me? Am I really not as smart as a fifth grader?

It took this happening a few times for me to realize that spatial recognition is a real strength for her. For me, not so much. I can do lots of things well, but spatial relationships are not one of them. The same holds true for Microsoft Excel. I can spend all day speaking to an audience, but ask me to create a spreadsheet and I'm done.

This doesn't mean we shouldn't spend any time developing our weaknesses. It simply means the time developing those areas should focus on keeping them from being a liability, rather than trying to be great at them. Ideally, it means using our strengths to develop our weaknesses.

A lot of us get caught in this trap. We compare ourselves to others. We consider others better parents or more supportive friends. We judge

Everybody is a genius. But if you judge a fish by its ability to climb a tree, it will live its whole life believing that it is stupid. —Albert Einstein

someone else as being more fun-loving or smarter than we are. We feel bad because they have a tidier house or a nicer car. We berate ourselves for not being "as good" as them.

Rather than spending all of our time and energy dwelling on fixing weaknesses, the real goal should be developing our strengths and leveraging them to take ourselves to a whole new level. What are you naturally good at? How can you use those strengths to excel? Are you highly extroverted and enjoy being surrounded by others? How can you use that strength? Are you detail-oriented, patient, and enjoy solving problems? How can you tap into that strength?

When we allow ourselves permission to develop our strengths rather than fixate on our weaknesses, we end up happier, more effective, and more successful. Had Rodney learned that, he could have been the next Energizer Bunny.

SLIGHT EDGE STRATEGY

- **List your strengths:** Make a list of all of the things you gravitate toward or that come easily for you. What are your greatest strengths? What can you do to spend more time developing them?

- **Write down your challenges:** Make a list of things that really challenge you. If you're a "runner" or "jumper," what are your "flying" and "swimming" attributes? What can you do to develop those to a point where they are not hindering your progress?

STRATEGY 45:
Boost Your Emotional Quotient

f I asked you to identify how someone was feeling simply by observing them, could you do it? How? By using the same skill that explains why some people atrophy while others thrive. It's why some people have lasting, meaningful relationships and others don't. It's a concept called Emotional Intelligence Quotient (EQ).

Emotional intelligence is defined as our ability to recognize and understand emotions in ourselves and others, and our ability to use this awareness to manage our behaviors and relationships. It determines how we make decisions, interact in social relationships, and how we relate to others. Those of us with a higher EQ are better able to form lasting, positive relationships, adapt to changing conditions in our environment, and be a positive influence on others.

Our Intelligence Quotient (IQ) is our ability to learn. Many neurologists would argue that it is fixed at birth and is not flexible. (This means we currently have the same capacity to learn as we did when we popped out of the womb. Comforting, huh?) Our EQ, however, is flexible and is a skill that can be learned. In essence, a high EQ can be developed even if we are not born with it. There is no known connection between IQ and EQ.

EQ accounts for 58 percent of performance in all types of jobs, and the link between EQ and earnings is so direct that every point increase in EQ adds approximately $1,300 to an annual salary. EQ is the single biggest predictor of performance in the workplace and the strongest driver of leadership and personal success.[23]

So how does EQ work? Basically, our brain stem filters our senses and puts them into the brain for processing. These messages go first to the

---

[23]Travis Bradberry and Jean Greaves, *Emotional Intelligence 2.0* (San Diego: TalentSmart, 2009).

amygdala—the emotional center of the brain—and then to the neocortex—the logical thinking part of the brain. Suffice it to say, we can't process our reactions to human interactions without an element of emotion; it's neurologically impossible. We have emotional reactions to almost everything that happens in our lives, whether we are aware of them or not. The more intense our emotions, the more likely they are to dictate our actions and behaviors.

What's Your EQ?

How can we harness the power of our emotions in order to get the most from ourselves and the people around us?

First, you have to assess your current level of EQ. There are myriad online assessments to choose from; simply Google "Emotional Intelligence Test." In essence, you must first be aware of your emotions and emotional responses, your traits, and the characteristics of your personality (what makes you unique). These include strengths, values, fears, beliefs, what you need from others, passions, etc.

Second, it's also helpful to know your triggers and blind spots. Triggers are those things that cause you to have a knee-jerk reaction that may or may not be the best reaction to a given situation. Blind spots are those areas of your personality and behavior that you are unaware of. Just ask someone close to you, they'll be happy to point them out (see Strategy 28). All of us have triggers that stimulate emotions such as anger, jealousy, embarrassment, and guilt, and all of us have blind spots.

Our brains are capable of becoming more emotionally intelligent over time as they continue to develop and form new connections. This process is called self-directed neuroplasticity (I touched on this in Strategy 5). We can learn self-mastery of our emotions if we take ownership and realize that we, and no one else, are responsible for our emotions. It takes a great deal of practice, willingness, awareness, and a constant commitment, but over time, we can form new habits.

We use emotional intelligence to connect with others. Do others believe you know and care about them? Do you listen attentively and truly empathize with people? These are the things that build emotional connections with others.

Use It or Lose It

Be aware of the mood you bring into the room when you show up. Is the room better when you enter or when you leave? How does your mood show up at work, and how does it affect the people around you? What percentage of your day are you happy, sad, angry, etc.? Make conscious decisions about how you're going to show up. Your mood matters. You get to decide the kind of mood you are in, and that mood will translate to the people you work and live with.

How can you accelerate your EQ? Become more self-aware, learn to master your emotions in the moment, practice making deep connections every day, and create a habit of being positive and optimistic with the people around you. Think about emotions that detract from your effectiveness (annoyed, angry, gloomy, anxious, fearful, nervous) as opposed to emotions that enhance your effectiveness (joyful, playful, inspired, adventurous, grateful, amazed, imaginative, cheerful). With awareness, commitment, and hard work, anyone can improve their EQ.

Just remember, if you want to be the person you have never been, you must do what you have never done before.

SLIGHT EDGE STRATEGY

- **Take an online EQ test:** Carve out some time without interruption to complete it.

- **Revisit your strengths and triggers:** Without knowing what your strengths are, you won't be able to leverage them to your benefit. What are your typical triggers? How do they affect how you react?

- **Pay attention to your emotions:** What percentage of the day are you in a "good mood" versus a "bad mood."

- **What can you do this week to build your emotional quotient?**

STRATEGY 46:
Remove Self-Imposed Barriers

More than one hundred years ago, scientists embarked on an experiment. Researchers put a northern pike, a fierce carnivorous fish that eats smaller fish, in an aquarium filled with minnows. At first, the pike was allowed to eat the minnows with reckless abandon. Then the scientists separated the pike from the minnows with a glass divider.

The pike began to repeatedly ram its head into the glass, making numerous failed attempts to eat the minnows. As time went on, the pike ultimately stopped trying to get the minnows. Slowly the pike learned that reaching the minnows was an impossible task, and simply gave up. The researchers then removed the glass barrier and the minnows swam freely around the tank. The pike stayed in one place and never tried to eat the minnows. Finally, it died of starvation. The study has been replicated many times since then, each time drawing the same conclusions. This has become known as the Pike Syndrome.

The Pike Syndrome is all too common in our everyday lives. We make assumptions or feel victimized by our environment, and we fail to push past our self-imposed barriers of limitation.

We often create these barriers with our assumptions. Maybe we have tried to go for a big promotion and didn't get it. Maybe we have tried to get fit or lose weight and haven't been successful. Slowly, after multiple attempts, we simply tell ourselves that we just can't do it, we give up, and slowly our dreams die.

We stay stuck, committed to the past, and this prevents us from moving with the tide of change. We have gotten to the point where we end up not even questioning our behavior. After all, this is our reality. We assume things can't and won't change.

I have certainly experienced the Pike Syndrome. I have been writing this book for more than six years. At the three-year mark, around the time

Evan was hospitalized, I came to the conclusion that it just wasn't going to happen. I had too much going on. I was speaking and consulting full time, managing all the realities of Evan's illness (which were completely exhausting), raising Rylee, maintaining my marriage, remaining a good friend and daughter, volunteering for NAMI, and more. I was spent, and I allowed myself to become defeated.

I gave up on my dream of writing a book and stopped believing it was even possible. A couple of years went by, the reality of Evan's situation didn't change, and neither did my other responsibilities. I was still busy and still spent. After reading about the Pike Syndrome, I realized that *I* was the problem. No one was telling me I couldn't do it. No one was trying to convince me that I didn't have what it takes, and no one was standing between me and a keyboard.

I slowly got a renewed sense of determination and wrote a little each day, making it part of my routine. Chapter by chapter, I began to break through my imaginary glass barrier, and I am so proud of myself for doing it. By no stretch was it easy. There were still days I wanted to give up, had thoughts of inadequacy, and shed tears. I eventually tore the barrier down, and you are now reading the fruits of my labor.

Are you a victim of the Pike Syndrome? Are you held back by an imaginary glass divider of your own making? Have you told yourself that this is just the way it is?

Your mind is ultimately in control of your actions and behaviors. You might be telling yourself that you are too old to change careers or go back to school, or that you aren't smart enough to try that new thing you've always wanted to try. You could be limiting yourself by your lack of self-confidence, your insecurities, and your doubts without even knowing it. Once our minds perceive a barrier exists—even if it isn't a real barrier or if the barrier has been removed altogether—we begin to believe it is there for good. We may not die of starvation, but we allow our dreams to slowly fade and eventually die.

I suspect we all fall victim to the Pike Syndrome in one way or another. Being aware is the first step. We all have self-doubt, we all have insecurities, and we all have that little devil on our shoulder that makes us question ourselves. Fortunately, we have the ability to break through those thoughts and assumptions, and although it takes some effort, it is possible.

Begin asking yourself some tough questions. What are the imaginary barriers of self-limitation in your life? Where have you told yourself that change just isn't possible, or it's not worth it to even try? What do you need to do to start swimming freely? For many of us, it's simply coming to the realization that we are holding ourselves back, and it's not some imaginary force beyond our control stealing the opportunity.

What have you wanted to do but have held back because you've believed it impossible? What have you wanted to try, pursue, or accomplish but haven't because your assumptions have dictated your behavior?

Once you identify these self-imposed barriers, you can start tearing them down. It may be a slow process, but it can happen. You can achieve your dreams. You simply have to get out of your own way.

SLIGHT EDGE STRATEGY

- **Identify self-imposed barriers:** Examine the situations in which you have fallen victim to the Pike Syndrome. Why do you think you limit yourself?

- **Destroy the barriers:** Pick one area and set a goal to begin tearing those barriers down. (Flip to Strategy 41 for more help on setting and accomplishing goals and use the Goal Planning Sheet in Strategy 42.)

STRATEGY 47: Take Care of Yourself

We all want to be more productive. Sometimes we forget that we're human and that we need more than just tips on how to trim the fat and go faster. We need to give ourselves permission to be human. If we forgo the things that recharge us, we won't be as productive, successful, or as happy as we can be.

Let Your Mind Wander

We're so busy focusing and moving our brains from one task to the next, we seldom take time just to think. How much time do you spend just thinking? Whether you call it creative thinking or introspection, take time each day and just let your mind wander. It is not a luxury. It is a necessity.

Breathe

While the alternative isn't a great option, most of us don't breathe correctly. We need to learn to breathe deeply, even if it's just for short intervals during the day. When you start to feel stressed, breathe in through your nose, hold it for four or five seconds, and breathe out through your mouth. Do this several times until you feel a little calmer. There are dozens of CDs, books, and programs that focus on guided meditation. This can be a great source of stress relief. Don't underestimate the power of breath.

Say Yes…and

Do you take other people's priorities on as your own? Do you find it hard to say no? If so, you may be letting other people sink your boat. I'm not suggesting you don't help others, but there is also a point where you have to focus on what you need. You are no good to anyone if you're exhausted and burnt out. If you have trouble saying no, try saying "yes… and." For example, if someone asks you to take on yet another task, you can say, "Yes, and I can do that as soon as I finish the current project" or "Yes, and does that take priority over what I'm currently working on?" A lot of people would say "yes, but." However, the word "but" evokes defensiveness and acts like a big eraser. "Yes, but I'm very busy right now" can become "Yes, and I'll be happy to help when I have a moment."

Stop to Refuel

We refuel our cars because if we didn't, they would fizzle out and go nowhere. Make sure you are just as kind to yourself. What is your fuel? Is it alone time, sleep, family time, exercising, eating well, or something else altogether? It's like in the movie *Cars* where Lightning McQueen thought he was so smart because he didn't waste time to stop and refuel. He was ahead for a while, but it finally caught up to him. We can only go so far on fumes. We need down time to think, breathe, and just be. We can't be everything to everyone. Give yourself permission to take a break and take care of yourself. Don't underestimate the power of eating well, exercising, and getting enough rest. They are game changers.

Laugh!

Many studies have shown that laughter relaxes the body, relieves physical tension and stress, boosts the immune system, triggers the release of endorphins, and actually helps your heart. Whether it is watching a funny movie, going to a comedy club, or sharing a funny story, laughter is great medicine. I credit standup comedians and stupid comedies for helping me survive the last decade.

Imagine Success

Imagine what success feels and looks like. Athletes use visualization to train because it has been proven to work. Formula One race car drivers and astronauts use simulators to teach their brains how to respond in a real situation. And it works!

When you focus on something, that focus creates thought patterns and ideas you wouldn't have had otherwise. It can create new neurological patterns. Visualizing success isn't some froufrou imaginary practice. There's scientific evidence that we can create our own reality with our thoughts.

Take Action

Just like you can't get thinner by watching others exercise, you can't accomplish your goals just by dreaming about them. Take action, even if you don't feel like it. If you wait for the magical moment to get started, you may be waiting a long time. Be like Nike: Just Do It!

Remove Self-Imposed Limitations

Do you remember Robert Downey, Jr. before he was Iron Man? He was a 1980s rising star who spectacularly fell from grace with his copious drug abuse. He only rebounded because he discovered his focus and changed his attitude. He lives by this simple philosophy: honor yourself. We are the ones who limit ourselves. Sometimes it's just a matter of getting out of our own way. Recognize self-defeating thoughts. Get a good handle on the negative messages you send yourself so that you will recognize them, dismiss them, and take action toward your goals.

Hold Yourself Accountable

If your boss told you to have a project done on time, you'd find a way to do it. You are the CEO of your life. If you don't create a system of accountability, no one else will.

Don't Derail

Remember, just because you get off track doesn't mean you have to completely derail. Forgive yourself and move on.

We need to give ourselves permission to be human.

SLIGHT EDGE STRATEGY

- **Know your needs:** Spend some time each day thinking not just about what you have to get done, but what you need as well. You need to breathe, to laugh, to say no, to be kind to yourself, etc.

- **Recognize self-defeating thoughts:** What are you telling your-self that is causing more harm than good? Put a stop to these thoughts as soon as you recognize them by replacing them with a more positive and realistic thought.

- **Visualize success:** Pick a task or outcome you would like to achieve. Close your eyes and visualize what success looks like. Practice imagining this in detail each day.

STRATEGY 48: Nix Negativity

No Complaints! No Problems! No Bad Moods! No Negativity! No Dumping!

What would happen if we put a sign like this outside our office, cubicle, bedroom, or house? What if for the next 24 hours we heard no problems, no complaints, no negativity, no venting, and no gossip? We would probably feel pretty darn good.

Can you think of the last time you went 24 hours without hearing any negativity or complaints, or the last time you went 24 hours without being negative or complaining?

Some people are just drawn to drama. They seem to absolutely revel in finding the most negative side of things. If it's raining, they complain about the rain. If it's sunny, they're worried about drought or heat. These people look for others with whom to commiserate. Feeling bad almost seems to feel good to them. Negativity feeds on negativity. If you've let yourself be the dumping ground for one of these people, especially if you commiserate, they'll seek you out over and over again. And you may find, if you pay attention to how you feel afterward, that your day seems a little dimmer, the world more hopeless, and your mood more sour.

I'm not talking about letting a close friend or loved one blow off steam once in a while. Everyone needs to do that. It's even okay to complain or be negative every now and then—life happens. I'm talking about people who always seem to have some misfortune or injustice to report. Some people just draw negativity to themselves.

Be Closed for Business

Some of us are rarely chosen as a dumping ground for the Negative Nellies. We communicate, through a blank face or nonresponse, that we're not open to that kind of conversation. Conversely, some people seem to be the go-to person for those who want to complain.

If you've let yourself be a dumping ground for a negative person, breaking the pattern won't be easy, but doing it is crucial to your own happiness. You'll have to gently and persistently let that person know you are "closed for business."

Chances are this person will not thank you for providing this new perspective. People who are engrossed in negativity often feel rejected and angry when others won't listen to their complaints. This is about them, and there's a good chance they won't change until they're really motivated from within. They've probably been that way for years. You don't have to stay locked in that place with them. Will they feel betrayed because you've suddenly put up a "No Dumping" sign? Probably. Do it anyway. They'll soon find another dumping ground, and you'll feel lighter, freer, and happier.

Whether you are a victim of letting other people dump their problems and negativity all over you, or if you are in the habit of dumping on yourself or others, follow these steps to get your 24-hour pass for a dump-free zone:

1. **Stop dumping on yourself:** Are you guilty of saying negative things to yourself about yourself? Do you find yourself thinking negative, self-defeating thoughts? Create a no dumping rule for yourself. Every time one of those thoughts comes into your head, yell at it, "No Dumping!" Make an effort to talk to yourself positively, rather than listen to any negative thoughts you may have. Be conscious of the messages you send yourself.

2. **Create a "No Dumping" sign:** Our brains respond to visual ques. If you want to remember to stay positive or create an environment of positivity around you, make a sign or get some other visual reminder that you'll see often.

3. **Stop enabling the dumping:** Remember, you train people how to treat you. If others are coming to you full of negativity, complaints, and drama, you have to ask yourself what you're doing to enable the behavior. Even just passively listening gives people the invitation to continue.

4. **Practice extreme happy:** You've heard of extreme sports? Practice extreme happy. Every time you head down a path of negativity, claw your way back to happy, kicking and fighting if you have to.

5. **Change the subject:** I've had people say to me, "Yeah right. When someone is complaining about something, what am I supposed to do, stop them?" Yes! Either gently change the subject, change the direction of the conversation, or move on. You get to choose what you listen to.

6. **Give yourself a "holiday":** If the thought of overcoming negativity, complaining, and dumping is too overwhelming, make up your mind not to engage in it for the next hour. Take baby steps.

7. **What's the payoff?** Every behavior has a reason. If you can't seem to escape the negativity, you have to start asking yourself what benefit you're getting from the behavior. Once you figure it out, find a different way to get what you need.

SLIGHT EDGE STRATEGY

- **Be aware:** Become aware of how many negative thoughts and conversations happen in your day. Keep track of them in a notebook or journal. The goal is to minimize the number as time goes by.

- **Seek the positive:** Start looking for a positive every time you have one of those negative thoughts. You don't have to become a Pollyanna, just break the knee-jerk reaction to thinking negatively.

- **Post a "No Dumping" sign:** Gently discourage "dumpers" from bringing negativity into your day.

STRATEGY 49: Improve Productivity with Different Behavior Styles

There's a lot we can do to maximize our own productivity. What do we do when we are dealing with other people? How do we draw the best productivity out of others? It goes back to understanding people's styles (see Strategy 30) and adapting to them, rather than expecting people to adapt to ours.

Increasing Productivity with Drivers

Remember Drivers? They're fast-paced and results-focused. They are big-picture thinkers who often overlook details. A Driver would prefer to get more done with a few errors, than take too much time and get it perfect.

Because Drivers process quickly, they often think they have communicated ideas that actually never left their own heads, and they feel frustrated that others just don't get it. (Hmm...sounds like that song experiment in Strategy 26, doesn't it?)

Drivers are impatient, easily frustrated, and like control. They often fail to delegate because they think they could get it done quicker, better, and easier. They prefer to work under pressure and often wait until the last minute to complete tasks and meet deadlines.

Here are a few strategies to improve your productivity when working with Drivers:

1. **Get to the point:** If you are writing an email that requires an action, include "Action Requested" in the subject line. Drivers zip through emails, and this will help separate the informative emails from actionable ones. Rather than write in paragraphs, use bullet points and attach more detailed information if necessary.

2. **Be on time:** It shows you have respect for their time and yours.

3. **Don't take it personally:** Drivers can be brusque, especially when stressed. It's how they function. It's not about you.

4. **Give options:** Drivers like control. Create some options you're comfortable with and let them choose. "Would you rather meet this afternoon or tomorrow morning?"

5. **Pay attention:** Drivers communicate impatience physically, with gestures like looking at their watches and tapping their feet. Either get to the point faster or ask if they would prefer to meet another time.

6. **Be solution-oriented:** When interacting with Drivers, be careful not to identify problems without suggesting solutions. Otherwise you are perceived as a whiner.

Increasing Productivity with Expressives

Expressives are also big-picture thinkers, fast-paced, and extroverted. They process quickly, bore easily, and tend to jump from task to task, often getting sidetracked.

Expressives are relationship-oriented and worry about looking bad in front of other people. They often refuse to delegate because they fear people will think they can't handle a task. They're emotional thinkers and sometimes make impulsive decisions that they regret. This leads to indecisiveness.

To improve productivity with an Expressive:

1. **Build Relationships:** Allow a few minutes before your business conversation for relationship building.

2. **Focus:** Help them remain focused by steering conversations back to the task at hand.

3. **Be nice:** Know that niceties are a big deal to Expressives. Take the time to write "good morning" in an email, rather than just jumping into facts.

4. **Be detailed:** Email with bullets and attach more detailed information if needed.

5. **Provide ideas for implementation:** Expressives have amazing and creative ideas but they struggle with implementation. Talking through strategies, challenges, issues, etc. will help them think through the process.

6. **Provide context:** Expressives are big picture thinkers and want to understand things in context. Start with the end in mind; then fill in the details. Explain the "why" behind requests.

7. **Show appreciation:** Expressives thrive on recognition and feedback. Without it, they are likely to disengage.

Increasing Productivity with Amiables

Unlike Expressives and Drivers, Amiables tend to be calm, patient, easygoing, and introverted. Amiables like harmony and peace, enjoy serving others, and dislike conflict, confrontation, and change. They let frustration build for quite a while before saying anything, but once they have reached their limit, they snap, and it is hard for them to get over it.

Because they do not want to be a burden, they often fail to delegate or ask for help, which can leave them feeling overwhelmed. Amiables are also indecisive, which can frustrate the other styles.

Amiables do not like to be put on the spot and prefer time to think through information and details. They like a lot of data, and they tend to be linear thinkers.

To improve productivity with an Amiable:

1. **Factor in relationship building:** Take time to build a relationship just as you would with the Expressive.

2. **Be detailed:** Give Amiables details and a chance to review the information and then provide time for questions and clarification.

3. **Don't embarrass or interrupt them:** If an Amiable makes an effort to contribute information, be patient, listen, and speak to

them privately if you disagree. Because Amiables process first, it's tempting for others to ask a question, get uncomfortable with the silence, and answer the question themselves. Just because Amiables may not be extremely assertive doesn't mean they have any less of a need to communicate their thoughts and ideas.

4. **Provide timelines with milestones:** It sometimes takes the detail-oriented Amiable longer to complete tasks. If they have clear expectations of deadlines and needed results, they will do everything they can to meet them.

5. **Pay attention to their nonverbal communication:** Amiables don't like conflict. If they are bothered by something, they are unlikely to confront you. Look at their body language and facial expressions. They speak volumes.

6. **Set them up to succeed:** Amiables enjoy working on a team and knowing they are making a difference. Amiables will go above and beyond if they feel valued and appreciated.

Increasing Productivity with Analyticals

Analyticals, like Amiables, tend to be slow-paced, detail-oriented, and methodical. Like Drivers, they're focused on results. They pride themselves on quality and thoroughness, and they enjoy solving problems.

Analyticals like to be in control and often resist delegation. They're perfectionists, so they need timelines to avoid "paralysis of analysis."

To improve productivity with an Analytical:

1. **Be on time:** It shows you have respect for their time and yours.

2. **Give details:** Like Amiables, Analyticals want a great deal of information. If you really want to make their day, put the information in a spreadsheet!

3. **Provide timelines with milestones:** Provide clear expectations of deadlines and needed results.

4. **Be patient:** Analyticals want and need time to process information and data. Do not rush a decision. Honor their methodical approach.

5. **Do your homework:** Be prepared to show you've really studied the information and, if you're trying to persuade them, show you've looked at both sides of the issue.

6. **Stick to business:** Analyticals are not as "touchy feely" as Amiables and Expressives. They prefer to focus on facts and results.

7. **Don't take it personally:** Analyticals may come across as skeptical or critical because of the way they probe and ask questions. Rather than get frustrated, recognize that they are gathering data and getting the details they need.

SLIGHT EDGE STRATEGY

■ **Identify the style of the people you work with:** This week, identify one to three people you frequently interact with in your personal and/or professional life. Write down ways you can improve those interactions and put them in to practice. Each day, stay focused on only one style (for example, Drivers on Monday, Amiables on Tuesday, Expressives on Wednesday, and Analyticals on Thursday). On Friday, see if you can manage all four of them!

■ **Modify your approach:** What can you do to modify your approach with others to get the desired outcome?

■ **When are you most productive?** Ask this question and share your answer with those you work with.

STRATEGY 50: Change Directions

If you do not change direction, you may end up where you are heading.—Lao Tzu

W e had the same boring beige paint in our house for a while, and it was time for a refresh. Jay and I agreed we wanted to try something new and contemporary.

After testing several samples, we decided to be risky and try a deep yellow. I left the painters to do their thing, and when I returned that afternoon, it looked like a banana had exploded all over our house. Not only was it the wrong shade, it was just plain wrong.

Sitting at the dinner table, we stared at our yellow walls. We had just spent our hard-earned money on a color disaster, and we were determined to make it work. We started brainstorming ways we could change the lighting, get creative with decorations, and shift the overall layout of the house to minimize the yellow.

As if we weren't miserable enough, we Googled yellow rooms only to find that they don't do well as main rooms of a house. Yellow, apparently, can stimulate feelings of frustration and anger. Interestingly, babies that have yellow rooms have been found to cry more than babies that don't. Given our situation with a highly oppositional and irritable child, it gave us both an ironic chuckle that we picked the one color that would not only fail to create a calming and peaceful environment, but that would exacerbate our already chaotic one! After a few days of lamenting, we realized that the cost of repainting was far less than spending the next several years frustrated by our banana of a house.

It may not be your house, but if something in your life has turned into a banana, it's not too late to make a change.

Give Yourself Permission to Change Your Mind

Are you living with a "banana"—a decision you've made that just didn't turn out like you had hoped? It's okay to be frustrated and disappointed that you have wasted time, energy, money, or all three, but it doesn't mean you have to be stuck with the decision.

You have the power and the ability to make conscious decisions about the course of your life every single day. The comforting truth is that for 99 percent of the decisions you are making, you can change your mind.

Give yourself permission to change directions, set different goals, shift your thinking, or start over. Every day, you can decide what you want your house, your job, your marriage, or your relationships to look like. While change is certainly not easy, it is possible. Don't limit yourself to the results you are getting from the choices you have made in the past.

So many times we make a decision to shift our course, but when we don't see immediate results, we revert back to what we were doing before. Change takes time. It's like planting a seed and expecting it to immediately grow into a tomato. We can't see what's happening under the soil, but every day subtle changes are taking place that will lead to the results we are after. We can stare at the soil every day waiting for that tomato to grow, or we can continue to water it and have faith that it will. Too many of us get frustrated with the lack of instant gratification, declare it a dud, and move on to planting different seeds.

Give your choices time to grow. Give yourself a chance to reap the fruits of your labor. Give yourself permission to dictate the direction of your life. After all, it is your life, and you get to choose what you want it to look like.

What choices have you made that didn't produce the results you were after? What has been holding you back from changing direction? Usually, the answer is fear. Remember Strategy 21? FEAR is simply False Evidence Appearing Real. Don't allow fear to dictate your life. I know—easier said than done—but if the result you are after is important enough, you will power through it.

I know for me, I'm often afraid to try new things for fear of failure. What if the choice was the wrong one? What if things don't go the way I had hoped? *What if…* It's the what ifs that slowly kill our passion, our energy, and our vision. So what if we fail? What if things don't go as we had hoped? What's the worst that can happen? Nine times out of 10, we simply make new choices, try again, and ultimately achieve the desired result. We wouldn't scrap a recipe because it didn't turn out perfectly the first time. We try again, adding a dash of this, changing an ingredient or two, and experimenting until we get it right. Life is no different.

Ironically, after literally sampling dozens of colors on our walls, we ended up with a nicer version of the beige we originally started with, and we appreciate it a lot more. Sometimes all it takes is a change in perspective to appreciate what we have. And sometimes it simply takes the courage to experiment.

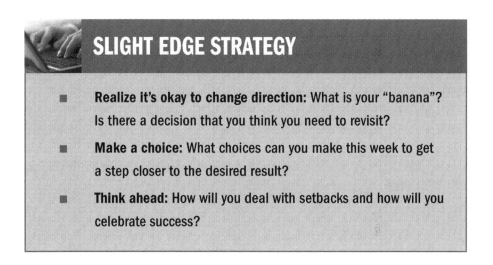

SLIGHT EDGE STRATEGY

- **Realize it's okay to change direction:** What is your "banana"? Is there a decision that you think you need to revisit?

- **Make a choice:** What choices can you make this week to get a step closer to the desired result?

- **Think ahead:** How will you deal with setbacks and how will you celebrate success?

STRATEGY 51: Take Charge of Change

Lately I've been asked quite a bit to speak on the topic of change, probably because technology—among other things—has accelerated the pace of change to the point where a lot of us feel we can't keep up with it. We feel dragged behind and pulled out of control. But technological change is only one kind of change with which we have trouble.

The only constant is change. Sometimes the change is one you hope for. Other times change will turn exactly in the direction you don't want it to. One way or another, things will change.

When it's a change we want, we have a tendency to pin all our hopes on it. We tell ourselves, "When _____ happens, I will be happy." Frequently, we then become frustrated that our lives didn't change as much as we had hoped. When it's a change we dread, we worry about it, grumble about it, and try to stop it from happening. Much of our effort to stop change from happening is futile; it only serves to make it that much harder to adapt.

I have seen this over and over again while raising Evan. I am initially fearful of change while hoping at the same time that every new pill or treatment will be the answer to help him get well. I've spent an inordinate amount of time pinning my hopes on what life could be when things change. I have had to conclude that while he will continue to change and grow, so will his illness. It might not be the change I want, but changes will continue to occur nonetheless.

Why do we struggle so much with change? Partly because we are wired to maintain the status quo. The oldest part of our brain, known

In the end it is important to remember that we cannot become what we need to be by remaining what we are.

—Max Dupree

as the reptilian brain, is hardwired to keep us safe, and the best way to stay safe is to travel familiar paths where we know there is no danger. So while we have to accept that change will come, we can also accept that change can be difficult and cut ourselves some slack.

Our danger is no longer the saber-toothed tiger. The danger we perceive is failure, loneliness, or the loss of something we hope for. When things change we have to think about how to function in the new environment.

Even the smallest changes can create anxiety. For example, when my grocery store got remodeled, I couldn't find anything, and I was frustrated because I had known where everything was. I could no longer zip through the store, ruminating about my day, running on autopilot, shopping for peanut butter. I had to concentrate on shopping, and I didn't want to.

When the change is a new job, loss of a job, a divorce, a move, or other big change, we have to rethink about how to live our lives. We have to concentrate on and plan things that used to be automatic.

Change brings the awareness that we are not in control. If we were in control, the only changes would be the ones we choose. We like a sense of having control of our futures, our environments, and our relationships. We live in a culture that's very big on having it "your way" and being "master of your fate."

Ironically, sometimes the best things in life evolve from changes we didn't want. People who lose their jobs, even jobs they're not that crazy about, go through a barrage of feelings—rejection, fear for the future, anxiety about their worth. Once they've moved through those initial feelings, those same people often decide to grab hold of the change and go after a job or a career that suits them much better. In the moment of going through change, it can almost feel like we are falling. If, however, we keep our eyes open for opportunity and expect good things to come of it, we fall into a much better place.

How do you manage all of the change that you experience regularly? Whether the change is at the individual, organizational, or community level, the same coping strategies apply. Here are a few things to consider when trying to navigate and manage the anxiety and upheaval that can sometimes come with change:

1. **Anticipate it:** Change is often difficult when we're caught off guard or frustrated that it's happening in the first place. Rather than assuming we're one project away from things settling down, expect that change will continue to take place.

2. **Be part of the solution:** Every change comes with opportunity. If you're looking for the opportunities, you can make the change better for everyone. If you resist change too much, you become part of the problem. You want to be part of the solution. Make time to figure out what you can do to support the change, rather than resist it.

3. **Fight evolution:** We are hardwired to resist change, but that doesn't mean it's impossible. Although our brains predispose us to maintain the status quo, we can manage change with focused attention and effort.

4. **Focus on what you can control:** Yes, you can influence others and situations, but the only things you have complete control over are yourself and your reactions. Don't waste time and energy trying to control external circumstances or people.

5. **Surround yourself with positive, productive people:** Have you ever been around a naysayer who is complaining about every part of the change? The people you associate with are a strong barometer of your success effort. Distance yourself from negativity.

6. **Manage your own morale:** Don't wait for others to motivate you or make you feel better. You must choose your own attitude and continually focus on renewing it.

7. **Reframe the way you're thinking:** More often than not, change brings about positive results. Rather than viewing the change as negative, reframe it as an opportunity. Remember, it is what it is and all you can do is all you can do.

SLIGHT EDGE STRATEGY

■ **Identify a recent change you have made:** How did you feel before, during, and after the change took place? What did you learn?

■ **Anticipate the next one:** When the next change comes (and it will), no matter how small, practice using the strategies above to embrace it.

■ **Become an agent of change:** What do you need to change to become a positive agent of change?

STRATEGY 52: Chart Your Course

When Jay found out he was getting laid off, I have to admit, I panicked. After all, he brings home a steady paycheck, handles the health insurance, and provides stability for our family. I immediately jumped into problem solving mode. Let's shore up the resume, go to networking events, start schmoozing, and make it happen! We don't have any time to waste!

While I was caught in problem solving mode, he did what very few people ever take the time to do. He stopped and asked himself, "What is it I really want?"

So many of us get caught up in the "practical concerns" that we don't take the time to dream or ponder the possibilities. I'm not suggesting you throw caution to the wind, forget the reality of your situation, and jump in blindly. What I am suggesting is a more balanced approach, using this as an opportunity to stop and proactively plan the next step rather than getting reactively sucked into it.

It's unfortunate that it usually takes the loss of a job, a midlife crisis, or some other major life changing event to get us to stop long enough and ask ourselves, "What is it I really want?"

The Practical Side

There is certainly the practical side of the equation. We have two kids—one who requires a significant amount of time, attention, and medical care. Although I know Jay would be great in a sales role, we both agreed that it would be too much stress on the rest of the family, trying to manage everything while he was traveling 50 to 60 percent of the time. Practical is important, but it doesn't have to eliminate the possibility of something amazing and fulfilling.

Identify the practical realities in your life that may affect your choices and decisions. List them on a piece of paper so you can see them. Be careful not to listen to the devil on your shoulder, and don't fall victim to the Pike Syndrome (see Strategy 46). Focus on the variables that cannot and most likely will not change, so you have a clear idea of what you are working with.

Then there is the more esoteric side. What do you really want? Have you always dreamed of opening your own business? Have you always wanted to find a way to turn your hobby into a profession? Do you want to go back to school? Learn a new skill? Change careers? Meet that special someone? Leave that someone who's not so special? If you weren't afraid you would fail, if you knocked down those imaginary barriers that were standing in your way, what would your best life look like?

How many times have you dreamed about that next chapter of your life but have been paralyzed to do anything about it because of the fear of lack: lack of money, lack of time, lack of courage. It's time to chart your course. Time is wasting, and you can't get it back. What are you going to do to take steps toward the life you dream about?

Dream Big

While practical thinking has its place, this is your opportunity to suspend judgment and not worry about the practical side of the equation. This is your chance to really let yourself brainstorm. Let your imagination soar. Let go of limitations and "what ifs." Imagine that you could be anything that you want to be, change any habits that are holding you back, and truly have a fulfilling career and life. What would you want? What would your perfect job look like? If money weren't an issue, what hobbies would you pursue? Don't limit yourself by what you *think* is possible. What do you really want?

Mingle the Ideal and the Practical

After you've given yourself some time (and it does take some time) to think about both the practical and the ideal, it's time to identify ways to mingle your ideal life with the very real practical obstacles. One by one, what can you do to reshape the way you are thinking, living, and operating so that you can find ways to turn your ideal scenario into reality? How can you chase your dreams, while still taking into account the practicalities of your life?

Go through the goal planning process we explored in Strategy 42. Then revisit the Goal Planning Sheet and identify your WIIFM. This is your motivation and is the key to accomplishing the goal. Next, list obstacles that could potentially stand in your way or prevent you from accomplishing your goal. These might be the practical concerns you previously identified. Now is the time to identify solutions (there are usually solutions to most problems). Finally, identify some very specific action steps with clear timelines. After all, a goal without a plan is simply a dream.

Spend some time asking yourself the tough questions. Give yourself permission to take the time to proactively plan your life, rather than simply doing what comes next. You don't have to be a hamster on a wheel. Your future and your life are in your hands. Make conscious decisions based on your goals, values, and priorities. Don't limit yourself with what ifs.

What are you doing today to get closer to the life you want? You can't do the same thing you've always done and expect to get a different result—that is the very definition of insanity. You will have to think differently, behave differently, and hold yourself accountable in ways you might have never done before.

Is it always easy? Of course not. Will it require some grit, sweat, and discomfort on your part? Only if it's worth doing. You, and only you, have the power to define the course of your life. Although you can't predict the future, you can define what you would like it to look like and work hard to make it a reality. After all, what you think about, you will bring about. Dare to dream big.

Riddle: Four frogs are sitting on a log. Three decide to jump off. How many frogs are left? Four. There's a big difference between deciding to do something and actually doing it.

This is your time. Stop deciding and start doing.

SLIGHT EDGE STRATEGY

- **Chart your course:** What do you really want? How do you get there?

- **Consider the practicalities:** What are the practical realities that need to be considered? Family, work, finances, dueling schedules—these are some of the things to consider.

- **Dream big:** If all of those limitations were gone, and you weren't afraid to fail, what would you do?

- **Take a chance:** What one step can you take this week to get you closer to accomplishing your dream?

Conclusion

Congratulations! Be proud of how hard you have worked to become more productive, positive, forgiving, and understanding of those around you.

I hope these 52 strategies have helped you on your journey toward becoming the person you envision yourself to be, just like they did for me. But don't stop now! Remember, the changes you've made for yourself are something you have to work at every day, every week. They don't just happen overnight and they won't stick around unless you invite them to stay. You have daily—sometimes even hourly—challenges in which you should keep using these strategies in order to overcome your life's obstacles.

You now have this great toolkit to help you tackle those curve-balls that life throws you—because rest assured, life's only constant is change. But now you're prepared. You live from your core values. You know how to handle difficult people or situations—or difficult people in difficult situations! You have given yourself permission to knock down your self-imposed barriers and to make adjustments to decisions that didn't quite work out the way you intended. You are courageous, resilient, and grateful.

If you feel like you're slacking back into your old, comfortable habits—the ones that weren't really doing it for you in the first place—then go ahead and revisit the wisdom within these pages. Look at your dream board. Find your inspiration again. It's under there somewhere! Courage lives within you, so if you stumble you know you have the bravery to try again tomorrow. Keep working your plan. But most of all, celebrate the changes you've already made!

Like I said at the beginning of this book—I have found that these 52 strategies bring order, peace, and happiness to my work life, my home life, my love life, and everything in between. I truly hope they do the same for you.

Epilogue

On November 29, 2010, we checked Evan into a pediatric psych hospital. After his discharge two months later, I was grateful that we would never have to go through that again. Until we did. Although he made definite progress after the hospital, he slowly regressed over time. On December 4, 2013, we made the gut-wrenching decision to check Evan into a residential treatment center. Were we right back where we started? No. We're smarter, stronger, and have better strategies to cope.

The day Evan was discharged from his second hospitalization—on February 5, 2014—I had a CT scan that revealed a parotid tumor in my face and neck. Later that month, I had a routine surgery to remove the tumor. Unfortunately, it wasn't that simple. After a six-hour surgery and the removal of an avocado sized tumor, the right side of my face was left completely paralyzed.

As if living with Evan's illness wasn't enough, I now had facial paralysis and was about to go through radiation to ensure the tumor didn't return, another surgery, and a life that will forever be impacted by checkups, tests, and treatments. This was not how things were "supposed" to go. I cried, felt sorry for myself, and cried some more.

Then I put on my big girl panties and got right back up. We cannot always control what happens in life, but we can most certainly control how we react and respond.

I won't be a victim, I won't stop searching for answers for Evan, and most importantly, I won't give up.

The 52 strategies outlined in this book will not fix every situation, they won't repair every relationship, and they won't solve all of your problems. They will, however, help you be happier, more productive, and more effective both personally and professionally.

I continue to focus on implementing these strategies every day. There is no "one and done" in this life. There is only taking one day at a time, doing what I can, and giving myself permission not to be perfect.

I can't know what the future holds for Evan or for our family, and I would be lying if I said I wasn't petrified. I will continue to pray for answers, I will continue to implement the strategies outlined in this book, and I will continue to learn new strategies. I won't borrow from tomorrow, I will stay present and mindful, and I will make conscious choices that align with my values. Will it be easy? I'm fairly confident the answer is no. It is what it is.

I love my family, and they are my number one priority. I will continue to be imperfect and will continue to make mistakes, but I will do everything in my power to rid myself of self-defeating thoughts, and I will choose to own my situation. I will care for myself as I would a loved one, I will embrace change, and I will conquer the FEAR that is holding me back. One day at a time.

Thank you for taking this journey with me. I hope this book has provided you with strategies, tools, and ammunition to live the life of your dreams.

Anne Grady Group

Would you like to have me speak to your team, group, or organization? To learn more, or to book a speaking engagement or team development session, visit my website at www.annegradygroup.com. I would love to know how this book has positively affected you! Send me your success stories at anne@annegradygroup.com or visit me online.

 www.annegradygroup.com/facebook

www.annegradygroup.com/linkedin

www.annegradygroup.com/youtube

www.annegradygroup.com/blog

@annegradygroup

National Alliance for Mental Illness

NAMI is a nonprofit organization dedicated to support, education, awareness, advocacy, and research to help those suffering with mental illness and the ones who love and care for them.

A portion of all book proceeds will be donated to NAMI to help further their goals.

For more information on mental illness, visit **www.nami.org**.

Made in the USA
Charleston, SC
23 February 2016